The Idiot's Guide to Quantum Physics

Understanding the Universe through Memes

by
Theodore Trudeau

Theodore Trudeau

Copyright 2024 Theodore Trudeau. All Rights reserved. No part of this publication may be reproduced without consent of the author.

Table of Contents

Chapter 1: Quantum Physics is for Everyone (Even You!)

Chapter 2: Schrödinger's Cat: The Quantum Dating Game

Chapter 3: Quantum Entanglement: Besties in Sync

Chapter 4: Quantum Physics in Media: A Cultural Lens

Chapter 5: Quantum Field Theory: Vibes and Energies

Chapter 6: Multiverse Theory: The Infinite You

Chapter 7: Quantum Mechanics for the Procrastinator

Chapter 8: Quantum Weirdness: Embracing the Chaos

Chapter 9: Quantum Physics as Life's Meme

Chapter 10: Trolled by the Universe

Introduction

Ever felt like understanding quantum physics was as likely as your cat suddenly speaking fluent Mandarin? Well, buckle up, because you're about to embark on a wild ride through the quirky world of quantum mechanics – and trust me, it's going to be a lot more fun than you think!

Let's face it, quantum physics has a reputation. It's that mysterious subject that makes most people's brains feel like they've been put through a blender. But here's the thing: it doesn't have to be that way. This book is your golden ticket to understanding the universe's weirdest secrets, all while having a good laugh.

Think quantum entanglement is complicated? Wait until you hear how it's basically just the universe's version of an inseparable bromance. And don't even get me started on Schrödinger's cat – that poor feline has been both alive and dead for so long, it's probably due for a mid-life crisis.

But why should you care about quantum physics? Well, for starters, it's the key to understanding how our universe ticks. From the tiniest particles to the vastness of space, quantum mechanics is the backstage pass to reality's greatest show. And let's be honest, who doesn't want to sound smart at parties?

So, forget everything you thought you knew about quantum physics being just for lab coat-wearing geniuses. This book is for you – the curious, the confused, and anyone who's ever wondered if they could teleport to avoid traffic (spoiler: you can't, but we'll explain why).

Get ready to laugh, learn, and question everything you thought you knew about reality. By the end of this journey, you'll be tossing around terms like "superposition" and "wave-particle duality" like a pro. And who knows? You might just find yourself falling in love with the beautiful absurdity of our quantum world.

Chapter 1: Quantum Physics is for Everyone (Even You!)

We've all been there—trying to wrap our heads around the principles of quantum physics while fighting off yawns or eye rolls. Imagine this: you're sitting in a lecture hall or scrolling through a physics blog at three in the morning, and the words start to blur together into an incomprehensible mix of letters and numbers. Concepts like wave-particle duality, superposition, and quantum entanglement seem to mock you, like a cat playing just out of reach. It often feels like you're trying to read a soufflé recipe in a foreign language while also climbing a mountain.

To lighten this intellectual load, let's unpack why quantum physics can feel so confusing. It's a field that often feels like a cosmic game of hide-and-seek, where the rules are slippery and everyone's dressed in bizarre costumes. When you first dip your toes into quantum mechanics, it's like wandering through a maze with shifting walls, creating new paths and dead ends at every turn.

One big reason quantum physics is so puzzling is that it turns everything we think we know about reality upside down. Traditional physics—the kind that explains everyday things like how a soccer ball flies through the air or how a car accelerates—works on principles that make sense to us. If you throw a ball, you can easily guess where it will land based on its speed and angle. Go ahead, try throwing a quantum particle and see where it ends up; I'll wait. Spoiler alert: you can't predict where it will land. Quantum mechanics introduces a whole new layer of uncertainty, and that's when things really start to get interesting.

Memes often do a great job illustrating this confusion. They're a visual reflection of the collective frustration that many experience with the subject. You might have seen the "Confused Nick Young" meme, featuring the basketball player with a look of total bewilderment. It perfectly captures that moment when quantum concepts hit you, seemingly defying all logic. "Wait, particles can be in two places at once?" is the kind of response that could easily accompany a screenshot of Nick's confused face. This reaction isn't just yours; even seasoned scientists have had their share of bewildering moments.

Let's take a moment to look back at the foundation of classical physics. Newton established the laws of motion and gravity, and for centuries, these principles guided our understanding. But when physicists began exploring the tiny world of atoms and particles, they found that the rules shifted entirely. For instance, the idea that a particle has a specific location or speed faded away, replaced by probabilities and uncertainties. It's like trying to play chess where the rules change every time you move a piece. That's the mental workout we're signing up for when we try to grasp quantum physics.

Consider superposition as an example. In the classic sense, an object is either here or there. But in quantum terms, it can be both here and there at the same time—until you actually look at it, of course. It's like when a friend texts that they're almost at your place, but you have no clue if they're still at home, halfway there, or somehow both places at once. This idea can twist your brain into knots, yet it's a core principle of quantum mechanics.

Now, let's explore quantum entanglement, a phenomenon that Einstein famously dubbed "spooky action at a distance." Imagine you have two socks in a drawer—one black and one white. If you reach in and grab one sock without looking, you instantly know the color of the other sock, no matter how far apart they are. But in quantum entanglement, it's like reaching into a drawer across the universe and still knowing the state of your sock. It's a bit like finding out your ex is dating someone who looks just like you—not only are you confused, but it feels like the entire universe is in on some cosmic joke that you missed.

Even the language of quantum physics can feel like a secret code that only a select few understand. Terms like wave functions, probability amplitudes, and quantization might seem like a jumble of jargon that requires a special decoder ring. The irony is hard to miss; we're trying to understand the fabric of reality, only to be met with words that push us further from clarity.

It's good to remember that even the brightest scientific minds have wrestled with these ideas. Richard Feynman, a giant in quantum mechanics, once quipped, "If you think you understand quantum mechanics, you don't understand quantum mechanics." If that doesn't give you some comfort about your own confusion, I don't know what will. The fact that the very creators of these theories find them baffling can reassure those of us feeling overwhelmed in a sea of quantum mysteries.

When you introduce quantum concepts to someone new to the subject, you'll often see reactions that range from curious to utterly bewildered. Friends might throw their hands up in frustration like they've just tackled a Rubik's cube blindfolded. "So, you're saying particles can communicate instantly across huge distances and exist in multiple states at once? How is that even a thing?" And you know what? That's a totally fair question. It shows just how wild our reality is, proving that we can't just slap a "Quantum Physics for Dummies" sticker on the topic and call it a day.

To make everything even more complicated, we also need to think about measurement. In quantum mechanics, looking at a particle forces it to "pick" a specific state. It's like playing hide-and-seek where you can't see your friend until you check under the right cushion. But as soon as you do, they're no longer hiding; they've made a choice, and just looking has changed everything. This opens the door to philosophical questions about how observation impacts reality—an idea that could make anyone's head spin faster than a particle in a collider.

On top of all this, quantum physics is packed with paradoxes. Take the famous double-slit experiment, for example. When particles pass through two slits, they can create an interference pattern, suggesting they're behaving like waves. But once you observe them, they act like particles, and the interference pattern disappears. It's as if they suddenly decide to be "appropriate" when they know they're being watched. This baffling behavior leaves many people scratching their heads and exclaiming, "This makes no sense!"

We also can't forget about Schrödinger's cat—a thought experiment that imagines a cat in a box that is both alive and dead until someone opens the box to check. Just imagine: you're about to unwrap a gift, and you're told that inside is either an adorable kitten or a rotting fish—until you look, both possibilities are true at once. What a way to turn an ordinary birthday surprise into an existential crisis!

As we wrestle with these ideas, it's helpful to keep in mind that confusion often leads to clarity. Even if quantum physics seems wild and absurd, it pushes us to rethink how we understand reality. It challenges us to broaden our perspective beyond classical physics and dive into the bizarre details of the universe.

In the grand scheme of things, the confusion surrounding quantum physics might not be a flaw but rather a feature. It reflects our natural curiosity and desire to explore the mysteries of existence. So, if you find yourself staring blankly at a textbook filled with strange symbols and equations, remember you're not alone. Each moment of confusion can be a stepping stone toward a deeper understanding of the universe.

Ultimately, while quantum physics may baffle and frustrate, it also enriches our view of what it means to be part of this incredible cosmos. Embracing the confusion might just be the first step toward uncovering the secrets hidden in the quantum world, where the impossible becomes possible and where the only certainty is uncertainty itself.

Wave-Particle Duality Explained

Let's take a moment to step into the quirky world of quantum mechanics, where particles are as unpredictable as that one friend who can't choose between binge-watching a show or hitting up a party. Here, we stumble upon a fascinating idea known as wave-particle duality. This concept has left scientists scratching their heads for years and has probably puzzled anyone who has ever tried to wrap their mind around it. To make things a little clearer—and maybe even a bit funny—let's draw a parallel from a place we all know well: the realm of modern dating apps. That's right, we're about to compare electrons to your latest Tinder match. Get ready!

Picture yourself swiping through profiles on Tinder. One moment, you come across someone who looks like a model, with perfect hair and a beach scene that screams, "I totally hike on the weekends." Swipe left? Not a chance! But as the conversation unfolds, you find out their chat skills are about as exciting as watching paint dry, and suddenly that picture-perfect profile feels like a well-polished illusion. Now, think about another potential match—someone who might look like they just rolled out of bed but can keep you laughing with their clever jokes for hours. This person radiates a wave of charm that you can't help but be drawn to.

Now, let's bring this back to the particles we learned about in school—specifically, electrons. Depending on the situation, they can act like that charming conversationalist or that overly-filtered model. In some experiments, electrons behave like particles, appearing in specific spots, while in others, they act like waves, spreading out as if they can't make up their mind about where to go. Just like dating, it seems electrons have dual identities, switching between two different forms based on how we observe them.

So, what's the big deal? Wave-particle duality tells us that particles aren't limited to behaving one way or the other; they can be both, much like we can take on different roles in our lives depending on the situation. This idea might sound strange, and honestly, it is. Yet, it points to a fundamental truth about nature and how we perceive reality. Just like that Tinder date who can flip from charming to clueless, electrons showcase their complexity.

Let's dig a little deeper into the science, but I promise to keep it fun. When we talk about particles acting like waves, we're referring to wave functions and probability distributions. In simple terms, these functions explain how likely it is to find a particle in a certain spot at a given time. Think of it this way: when you meet someone on a dating app, you get a vague idea of who they are from their profile, but until you actually talk, you're left guessing about their true self. Similarly, electrons follow their probabilistic wave functions, giving us a peek into their potential presence without pinning them down to a specific place until we measure them.

Ah, the measurement! That moment of truth—the equivalent of that first awkward conversation that can either spark a connection or make you wish you'd swiped left. In the world of quantum physics, measuring a particle is a game changer. When we observe a particle, it seems to 'choose' whether to be a wave or a particle, collapsing from a beautiful wave of possibilities into a single outcome. It's just like when you finally meet that Tinder match in real life; they might turn out to be even more charming than their profile suggested—or maybe not.

The famous double-slit experiment perfectly illustrates this duality. In this experiment, electrons are shot through two slits, creating an interference pattern on a screen behind them, which is the wave-like behavior. However, when we see which slit the particle goes through, that interference pattern disappears, leaving just two distinct lines on the screen—like the two paths your date could take: charming or awkward. The act of observing forces the electrons to pick a path, much like how a first date can set the tone for a blossoming relationship.

So, what's the takeaway? Just as each Tinder match has layers waiting to be uncovered, so do the particles in the quantum world. They aren't just one thing or the other; they embody nature's complexities, shifting their identities based on how we interact with them. This duality challenges us to rethink our understanding of reality and nudges us toward the idea that certainty isn't always attainable. The universe, it turns out, thrives on ambiguity, much like those cryptic text messages we get from potential partners.

As we embrace this wave-particle duality, let's also find the humor in the absurdity of it all. Life, love, and quantum mechanics seem to dance to the beat of uncertainty—where things can shift in an instant, and what we think we know can be turned upside down. When you really think about it, isn't it beautifully poetic that particles, much like ourselves, are multi-dimensional beings showcasing different behaviors based on how we choose to observe them?

Now, let's chat about what this duality means beyond our dating app experiences.

Understanding wave-particle duality has amazing consequences for technology and how we interact with our surroundings. Take quantum computing, for instance; it relies on these principles to process information in ways that traditional computers can only dream of. Being able to exist in multiple states at once allows quantum bits, or qubits, to perform calculations at lightning speed, potentially transforming everything from cryptography to drug discovery.

What's more, wave-particle duality has given us a deeper understanding of light itself. Light behaves similarly, showing both wave and particle traits. When we shine light on something, we're not just illuminating it; we're inviting a complex interplay of behaviors to unfold. Photons, the particles of light, can create interference patterns and still hit surfaces as individual packets of energy. So, the next time you snap a selfie with that overly-filtered Tinder model, remember that the very light capturing that moment is a manifestation of wave-particle duality—a wonderful mix of possibilities.

We also need to think about the philosophical implications of this duality. If our observation can change how particles behave, what does that mean for our reality? Are we, as observers, shaping the world around us just by being present? This idea has echoed through philosophy, from the ancient Greeks to modern thinkers, prompting us to question the very nature of existence. And just like a first date can influence the dynamics of a relationship, the act of observing can fundamentally change our reality.

In the end, wave-particle duality reminds us that life is full of contradictions. Whether in the quantum realm or in our daily lives, we often find ourselves navigating a sea of complexities. Our efforts to categorize and box things up neatly often meet with pushback. Just like we can't label people based solely on their profiles, we should accept that the universe is multi-dimensional, with layers waiting to be explored.

So, the next time you swipe through profiles or ponder the mysteries of the universe, keep in mind that both dating and quantum physics are filled with delightful uncertainties. Embrace the ambiguity and stay open-minded. As we learn to appreciate wave-particle duality in the quantum world, let's also recognize the dualities in our lives, acknowledging that our experiences are rich, nuanced, and constantly evolving. The universe, after all, is one grand, intricate dance of possibilities, much like the wild and unpredictable world of dating. If anything, it simply shows us that some of the most fascinating aspects of existence arise from the beautiful interplay of contrasting identities.

Schrödinger's Pizza

Imagine, for a moment, your favorite Saturday night ritual: the warm scent of cheesy goodness filling the air, the cozy glow of your favorite TV show lighting up the living room, and the excitement of waiting for that perfect pizza to arrive at your door. You've just called up your favorite pizza place, placed your order, and now the waiting game begins—a game that, much like the puzzling world of quantum mechanics, is full of uncertainty.

Now, let's add a fun twist to our pizza journey. What if I told you that until you check on your pizza, it exists in a state of superposition? Yes, that's right! Just like Schrödinger's famous cat, which is both alive and dead until someone looks, your pizza can be both delivered and undelivered, hot and cold, mouthwatering and frustratingly out of reach. It's a quirky idea, but stick with me as we slice through this analogy, and I promise you'll never see pizza—or quantum mechanics—the same way again.

Picture this: you're lounging on your couch, binge-watching your favorite show, and it hits you—it's time to treat yourself to that perfect pizza. You place your order and then sit back, ready for the deliciousness to unfold. But as the minutes tick by, you start to feel that familiar uncertainty creeping in. Did the delivery driver leave the restaurant? Did they take a wrong turn? Has your pizza vanished into the vast abyss of the universe? At that moment, your pizza is in a state of superposition, sitting in two contrasting situations: it's both on its way to you and not on its way to you.

It's a mind-bending thought that reflects the core idea of quantum superposition. In the tiny world of quantum physics, particles can exist in multiple states at once until we take a look at them. For instance, an electron can be in different spots at the same time, slipping in and out of existence, much like your pizza could be racing through traffic or sitting idle in the backseat of the delivery car, getting cold. It's a delightfully absurd notion that a simple food order can represent such a complex principle of science.

Now, let's break this down a bit more. The moment you decide to check on your pizza's status, similar to opening Schrödinger's box, everything shifts. You pull out your phone, open the app, and when you hit refresh, you're faced with the undeniable truth—either your pizza is indeed on its way, or it's still hanging out at the restaurant. In that split second of realization, the superposition collapses into one clear state. If the app shows that your pizza is on its way, fantastic! The joyful anticipation transforms into a mouthwatering reality. But if the app says it's still at the shop, your heart sinks just a little.

In quantum physics, measuring a particle works the same way. An electron floats in a cloud of probabilities, described by a wave function, until we observe it. Once we measure it, it "chooses" a position, leaving behind all the endless possibilities for one specific outcome. This idea isn't just a fun thought; it shapes how we understand the universe. The observations we make don't just reveal the properties of particles; they also actively affect their states. Our very act of peeking into the box determines the reality we see, just like checking the status of our pizza decides whether we can dive into our meal or feel a bit let down.

But wait, let's put the science aside for a moment. Think about the sheer joy of pizza. The thought of that first gooey slice is enough to make anyone smile. When we place an order, we picture the perfect pizza—its crust golden and crispy, the cheese bubbling and melty, and toppings like a treasure trove of flavor. Whether it's pepperoni or a veggie delight, the excitement stays the same. In that moment of uncertainty, we're filled with hope and joy, much like scientists are when they contemplate the countless possibilities found in quantum states.

This playful analogy has a deeper meaning too. Once we've observed the pizza's status, it reflects our choices. If you find out your pizza is on its way, you may feel thrilled, ready to dig in. But if it's still undelivered, you're faced with a choice. Do you wait patiently, hoping for the best, or do you channel your inner detective and call the restaurant to track down your pizza? This mirrors the implications of observing quantum phenomena. Our questions drive our discoveries; the act of seeking knowledge helps us uncover the nature of reality.

Of course, anyone who has ever ordered pizza knows that the delivery process isn't always smooth. There can be mix-ups, delays, or even the dreaded wrong order. Imagine the frustration of finding out your pizza has gone rogue, lost somewhere in the labyrinth of your city. This feeling of helplessness reflects the uncertainty at the heart of quantum mechanics. Much like our pizza can become a ghostly presence until we check on it, quantum particles can be elusive, darting around, teasing us with their unpredictable nature.

And let's not forget what happens when the pizza finally arrives. The delivery person knocks on your door, and suddenly, everything comes rushing back into focus. You greet them with eager anticipation, but as you reach for the box, you must confront the reality of what awaits you inside. This moment of unboxing your pizza is similar to the act of observation in quantum mechanics. It's at this point that all the possible flavors and toppings come together into one definitive pizza—maybe it's your favorite, or perhaps a surprise you didn't expect, forcing you to deal with the unexpected.

In life, just as in quantum systems, we often face the results of our observations. We can hope for one thing and end up with another entirely. Yet, this unpredictability is what makes life—and quantum physics—so fascinating. How many times have we longed for things to turn out a certain way, only to find ourselves facing an entirely different reality? Just like biting into a slice of pizza that mysteriously turned out to be anchovy and pineapple instead of the classic pepperoni, life offers us surprises that challenge our expectations and push us to adapt.

  Moreover, let's not overlook the joy of sharing a pizza with friends. The communal experience of enjoying pizza stands in delightful contrast to the solitary wait for delivery. When you gather around a table, sharing stories and laughter over slices of gooey goodness, the anticipation transforms into a shared experience. In this way, the pizza becomes more than just food; it turns into a symbol of connection and friendship.

  This idea of sharing resonates in the quantum world too. The entanglement between particles is like sharing a pizza with someone. Once particles become entangled, their states become linked, meaning that measuring one affects the other, no matter how far apart they are. Just as you might find yourself surrounded by laughter and the aroma of pizza, entangled particles dance through the universe, their fates intertwined in the fabric of reality.

So, the next time you're placing a pizza order, take a moment to appreciate the delightful absurdity of it all. The waiting, the anticipation, and the eventual checking of the delivery status—all these moments create a rich experience of uncertainty, excitement, and connection. In the whimsical world of quantum mechanics, just like in the ordinary act of waiting for pizza, we learn how to navigate the complexities of existence.

Embracing the idea of Schrödinger's pizza opens up a fun conversation about the nature of reality. It reminds us that uncertainty is a natural part of life—a tasty flavor we must learn to enjoy. Whether you're pondering the mysteries of the universe or just waiting for your favorite pizza to arrive, the lessons of superposition encourage us to embrace the unknown while finding joy in the connections we make along the way.

So, as you think about your next pizza night, remember it's not just about the delicious slice waiting for you; it's about the delightful journey that gets you there. Each order is a new adventure in a world full of possibilities, much like the quantum realm, buzzing with particles existing in states of superposition. And in our quest for understanding, we can find humor in the absurdity of it all, where pizza and physics come together in an unexpected yet delicious harmony.

Chapter 2: Schrödinger's Cat: The Quantum Dating Game

Imagine this scenario: a tightly sealed box, and inside, a cat is curled up and hidden away. At first glance, this might seem like the start of a quirky magic trick or perhaps a strange choice by a pet owner. But believe it or not, this setup is actually at the heart of one of the most famous thought experiments in quantum physics—Schrödinger's cat. Before you roll your eyes and think this is just another confusing scientific puzzle, let's unpack how this unusual story connects to the world of modern dating.

In the strange world of quantum mechanics, there's an idea that until we actually look, particles can exist in a kind of limbo—where they are both here and there, alive and dead, all at the same time. When Schrödinger first came up with this thought experiment, he was trying to showcase the weirdness of quantum theory. But let's be honest: all this talk about particles and states can be pretty confusing. So, let's break it down into something we all know—dating.

Picture yourself swiping through a dating app, your fingers moving quickly across the screen as if you're a scientist analyzing complex wave functions. Each swipe brings up a new potential match, each one a mystery just waiting to be discovered. Some profiles shout "I'm the one for you!" while others quietly scream "stay away!" But until you take that leap and start a conversation or—gasp—agree to meet for coffee, those potential partners are stuck in a state of uncertainty. They're both exciting and scary, charming and puzzling, much like that little cat in the box.

Let's take a moment to think about a typical dating encounter. You match with someone whose profile could fool even the most experienced catfish. Their bio is a dream: "Adventurer! Food lover! Bookworm! Can quote the most obscure movie lines!" With every detail, you can't help but imagine evenings filled with laughter and thrilling adventures. Yet, doubt creeps in. Are they really as amazing as they seem? Is this profile just a cleverly crafted façade, a shiny mirage in the endless desert of dating?

In the language of quantum physics, they are both the soulmate you've been dreaming of and a complete flop. You can picture that cat in the box, fur all ruffled and tail twitching, caught between happy purring and an angry hiss. Until you make a move, until you lift the lid off that box, you stay in a state of romantic uncertainty. How delightful—and how incredibly frustrating!

So, you gather your courage and send a message. "Hey there, fellow foodie! What's your favorite dish to cook?" You hit send, heart racing as you wonder what might happen next. Will they respond with excitement, sparking a connection, or will they leave you hanging, feeling as forgotten as stale leftovers?

Now here's where it gets interesting. Just like an electron that can be in many different states, your potential partner is now in limbo. Until they respond, they are both "into it" and "not interested." You can almost see Schrödinger's cat peeking through the box, full of possibilities, ready to jump into whatever adventure lies ahead. And let's be honest—when it comes to dating, we often find ourselves in a tricky spot, trying to decide whether to take a chance or stick to what we already know.

As you keep swiping, you start to notice a pattern. Many profiles proudly display the same qualities—adventurous, spontaneous, and, of course, "looking for a partner in crime." But we all know the dating scene is filled with the quantum equivalent of particles that are neither here nor there. They could be the life of the party or just another cat in a box, waiting for someone to open it and reveal the truth.

And here's the funny part. The dating world, much like quantum physics, is loaded with uncertainties. We find ourselves swiping right on people who promise connection and romance, but often the reality is as unclear as a barely opened box. In this online world, catfishing has reached new heights, with people curating their profiles like scientists preparing grand experiments.

Remember that meme that floated around a while back with a cat peeking out of a box, captioned "When you're waiting to see if your date shows up or if you're just dating a picture?" It perfectly sums up the feeling. The anticipation leading up to a first date fills us with both excitement and anxiety. As we sit in a café or bar, we face a big question: will the person across from us match the image we've built in our minds?

Just as particles can settle into a clear state when we observe them, our dating options can also come into focus when we finally meet someone. When that moment arrives, we navigate the tricky space between our hopes and reality. The ups and downs of dating can feel like a whirlwind of quantum shifts, where one minute you're filled with optimism, and the next, you're questioning every choice that brought you to this point.

Think about it: you finally meet your date, and they walk in looking nothing like their profile picture. Perhaps they've used clever angles and filters to present an idealized version of themselves. In that moment, you're not greeted by Schrödinger's cat, but rather an elaborate illusion—a hologram of the perfect partner. The box is opened, and like that cat, the truth is far from what you expected.

Yet, this is where the analogy takes an interesting turn. Just as quantum physics teaches us to accept uncertainty, maybe our approach to dating should reflect that same attitude. As we navigate the twists and turns of love, we need to be prepared for delightful surprises and, at times, disappointing letdowns. The key is to stay open-minded and curious, even when things don't turn out as we hoped.

Ultimately, dating—like quantum science—is all about probabilities. We swipe, we chat, we meet, and with every interaction, we get closer to understanding the true nature of our potential partners. Just like physicists observe particles to uncover their states, we too must engage with the people we meet to reveal the wonderful or disappointing truths hidden in that metaphorical box.

So, what's the takeaway? Life—and love—are filled with unknowns. Just like Schrödinger's cat, we learn to embrace the chaos and find joy in the unpredictable. After all, the universe is packed with wonders waiting to be discovered, and if that means taking a leap into the dating world, then so be it. In this grand adventure of love, let's keep our hearts open, our expectations balanced, and our sense of humor handy. Because you never know—you might just find a furry companion instead of a lifeless disappointment.

Quantum Uncertainty and Relationships

Imagine wandering through the often confusing maze of modern dating, with just your smartphone and a dash of hope as your guide. Welcome to a world where uncertainty is the name of the game, reminiscent of Heisenberg's famous idea that there are certain things we can never know for sure. Just like in quantum mechanics, where particles dance in a swirl of possibilities, our love lives are filled with twists and turns we can't always predict. In this new dating landscape, the fleeting nature of human connections can feel like trying to guess where a molecule might land.

Let's paint a picture that feels all too familiar. Picture yourself getting ready for a date, scrolling through a dating app, your heart racing with each potential match you come across. It's a bit like running an experiment—every swipe reveals new possibilities, each profile a different set of outcomes. Maybe one person is a fitness buff eager to drag you into a 6 a.m. spin class, while another is an intellectual who loves obscure documentaries and has a soft spot for cats. At this point, your options are as unpredictable as particles in a quantum state, full of possibilities based on the choices you make next.

If Heisenberg were to analyze the dating habits of millennials, he'd have plenty to say. The uncertainty principle shows up here when we think about the dual nature of our interactions. We're drawn to the idea of love yet terrified of rejection. Just reaching out can change everything; a simple "Hey, how's it going?" might kick off a chain reaction, turning a world of possibilities into one definite outcome. In that moment, you're both hopeful and anxious, excited and nervous.

And let's embrace the humor that often comes with this emotional rollercoaster. Dating in a tech-driven world means we feel a lot of pressure to send the perfect message. Have you ever spent way too long crafting a response, only to wonder later if you've completely overthought a simple "What's up?" It can make anyone question their sanity. You hit send, and suddenly you find yourself staring at your phone, refreshing your messages like a scientist peering through a microscope, eagerly waiting for a response. Until they reply, they exist in a state of uncertainty—both intrigued and uninterested, much like Schrödinger's cat in its mysterious box.

Then there's the first date—the big experiment that could lead to a budding romance or a total flop. You've spent hours deciding what to wear, imagining all sorts of scenarios, and rehearsing your lines. Will they find your jokes funny, or will you be met with awkward chuckles and uncomfortable silence? Just like how observing a particle can change its state, the vibe in the room shifts the moment you meet face-to-face. The anticipation is thick, and every little detail—your laughter, your gestures, the way you sip your drink—can tip the scales of attraction one way or the other.

It's a delicate dance where a misstep can send you spiraling into the abyss of "this isn't going to work."

As you sit across from your date, you might realize that this person doesn't quite match the image you had in your mind. Their profile picture could be from three years (and three hairstyles) ago, or they might have quirks you never expected. The dating world can be fickle, where the thrill of matching can quickly turn into uncertainty once you meet the real person sitting in front of you.

And let's not overlook the delightful mayhem that is dating apps. Swiping through profiles often feels more like a game show than a serious hunt for love. Imagine a host announcing, "Here comes our next contestant! They love hiking, cooking, and have a collection of novelty socks!" The stakes feel high, and you want to make a memorable impression. But just like quantum particles can behave unexpectedly, so can the reactions of those you meet. Will they be charmed by your humor, or will they decide you're more of a "swipe left" kind of partner?

In a lighthearted spirit, let's appreciate the comedic pressure to impress. On a first date, your mind races with thoughts on how to show your best self while trying to seem effortlessly cool. You might wonder, "Should I mention my love for collecting rare stamps, or stick to the basics?" Spoiler alert: sharing too much too soon is often the enemy of a good first impression. The dating scene is full of uncertainty that feels like trying to solve a Rubik's Cube blindfolded.

Now, think about the subtlety of online communication. Texting has turned into a modern art, where the clever use of emojis can make or break a conversation. One wrong move—like a misplaced winky face—and you could find yourself stuck in dating limbo, pondering if you read too much into their "LOL." The absurdity of such situations is bound to make you chuckle. "Did they mean 'I'm really into you' or 'Wow, that's...nice'?" This kind of ambiguity can feel like trying to pin down a particle's position and speed at the same time—good luck with that!

Still, among this delightful chaos, there's a significant truth: uncertainty can be both a burden and a breath of fresh air. The unpredictability of dating invites us to embrace the unexpected and engage in emotional exploration that leads to growth and self-discovery. Many of us have experienced awkward moments that, looking back, make for the best stories. That date that ended in a minor disaster—maybe an accidental spill or a forgotten wallet—can transform into a cherished memory, reminding us that life should be enjoyed, even when it doesn't go as planned.

Over time, relationships have taught us valuable lessons that reach beyond just romance. Whether it's dealing with a breakup or learning to communicate better with a partner, each experience helps us understand ourselves and others more deeply. Just like quantum mechanics nudges us to accept uncertainty, dating teaches us resilience. Every misstep and panicked moment paves the way for growth and connection.

In this digital age, where swiping and texting dominate our love lives, having meaningful conversations can often feel like an uphill battle. Yet, it's in those moments of vulnerability, when we allow ourselves to be real, that true connections start to blossom. As we open up and let our authentic selves shine through, we create space for love to flourish—much like how particles settle into a clear state when they are observed.

By embracing the uncertainty of dating, we can turn our experiences into an adventure rather than a stressful task. We begin to appreciate the little things, like late-night chats that stretch into the early hours or spontaneous road trips to nowhere in particular. With each encounter, we gather insights—information that may seem chaotic at first but ultimately helps us understand what we truly want in love.

The beauty of romantic uncertainty extends to the many ways we connect with others. Relationships aren't always straightforward; they can twist and turn, leading us down unexpected paths that result in delightful surprises. Sometimes, the person you least expect can become your greatest ally, turning a chance meeting into a lasting friendship. It's during these serendipitous moments that we discover the true magic of connection.

In simpler terms, life and love are all about finding joy in the unpredictable. Just as quantum mechanics pushes us to rethink our understanding of reality, dating encourages us to engage with the unexpected, challenging us to adapt and grow. Just like particles behave in ways we don't always expect, love often unfolds in surprising ways, leading us to moments of true beauty.

So next time you find yourself staring at a blank text screen or gearing up for a first date, take a moment to appreciate the uncertainty that comes along with it. Remember that you are not just a bystander in your romantic life; you are actively participating in a grand experiment where the possibilities are endless. With each interaction, you are crafting a unique story, filled with laughter, learning, and a hint of chaos.

Ultimately, it's not about knowing every detail or having the perfect plan; it's about staying open to whatever life throws your way. After all, in the grand scheme of things, relationships are a journey of exploration, discovery, and sometimes the hilarious misadventures that come with it. Like Schrödinger's cat, we're all learning to navigate life's uncertainties, embracing the chaos and finding joy in the delightful unpredictability of love.

Breaking Up with Schrödinger's Cat

Ah, the breakup—an experience that's both heartbreaking and surprisingly funny. It's a journey we all go through in our romantic lives. Think of it like Schrödinger's cat, a thought experiment that challenges us to face tough truths about life and death. Instead of a box, though, we're stuck in a relationship that feels tightly sealed by uncertainty. Just like that cat exists in a strange state of being both alive and dead, there comes a point in our own relationships when we realize they're hanging on by a thread, ready to slip away.

As you navigate this maze of feelings, keep in mind that the heart of a breakup is often the simple act of opening that box. Too often, we cling to relationships, hoping something—anything—will change for the better. It's like peeking into that box, half-hoping the cat will jump back to life, while deep down, we know it's time to face the facts. The relationship has flatlined, and it might just be time to let go.

When uncertainty looms, clear communication is your best friend. There's a certain strength in being honest that can cut through the fog of confusion. You might feel tempted to tiptoe around the subject, waiting for a "perfect moment" that never comes. But let's be real—when is there ever a perfect time to break up? Spoiler: there isn't. The longer you wait, the more the situation festers, and soon you'll find yourself stuck in a cycle of emotional limbo. You might catch yourself thinking, "I'm just waiting for the right moment to share my feelings," while secretly questioning if the cat in your relationship is still alive or already curled up on the couch, dreaming of happier times.

Self-reflection is also a key part of this emotional puzzle. Understanding why a relationship isn't working can light the way forward. Maybe you've stopped laughing at each other's jokes, or your conversations have turned into long debates about pineapple on pizza. Whatever the reason, it's crucial to recognize that relationships should uplift us, not bring us down. Taking a moment to reflect is like gathering your thoughts before a science experiment. You need to jot down your ideas about what went wrong and why, then take a step back to look at the bigger picture. Did you grow apart? Were your values mismatched? Or did you just discover that your partner thinks "Friends" is overrated? As painful as these realizations can be, they'll guide you toward a brighter future, allowing you to rise from the ashes of your relationship like a phoenix that knows exactly what it wants.

A lighthearted way to tackle this introspective process is to think of it like a relationship autopsy. Grab your metaphorical scalpel and dissect what went wrong, even if it means revisiting some cringeworthy moments. This can lead to laughter if you allow yourself to see your past relationship through a humorous lens. Picture yourself sharing that one time your partner believed your Netflix obsession was just a phase, or the weekend you spent binge-watching a series they had zero interest in—only to have them walk in on you crying over a fictional character's fate. Turn these experiences into funny stories that not only highlight the silliness of love but also serve as lessons for future relationships.

    As you navigate the emotional rollercoaster of a breakup, remember to embrace your resilience. Heartbreak is a shared human experience, much like the collective sigh of every cat owner whose feline friend just knocked over a carefully arranged vase. If you've been contemplating the breakup for a while, you've probably already felt the sadness and frustration tied to it. So, in many ways, actually breaking up can feel like shedding a heavy weight, bringing you closure and letting you finally breathe after being stuck in a cycle of uncertainty.

You might find solace in leaning on friends and family who have weathered their own storms. There's something comforting about gathering around a table with your closest buddies, swapping absurd breakup stories. Share the tales of dramatic "It's not you; it's me" speeches, the awkward moments when someone accidentally called their ex during a heated argument, or the classic "we can still be friends" line that often leads to weird Thanksgiving dinners. These stories remind you that you're not alone in this chaotic experience and that even the toughest moments can become oddly funny with time.

While you're at it, let's add a bit of humor about the ridiculousness of trying to hold onto a relationship that feels lifeless but hasn't officially ended. Imagine still texting your partner despite knowing that the spark has long fizzled out. It's like keeping a wilting plant on your windowsill, watering it every Sunday, hoping it'll come back to life one day. But here's the reality check—sometimes, it's better to let go and clear the way for a fresh start. Maybe it's time to indulge in a little metaphorical spring cleaning. Toss out those half-hearted texts, delete the inside jokes that no longer make sense, and give yourself permission to move on.

Just like Schrödinger's cat, there will come a moment when you need to assess the situation and accept the outcome. You might feel tempted to linger in that state of uncertainty, but it usually leads to nowhere good. You've got to open the lid and face the fact that the cat isn't just napping; it's very much gone. This moment of clarity can be freeing, so don't shy away from it. The goal isn't to rush into a breakup with chaos but to approach the conversation with kindness and understanding. Though it's tough, expressing your feelings can open the door to healing and clarity.

After the breakup, you might find yourself in a world that feels both familiar and strange. The dating landscape may change, but each stumble and recovery teaches you something valuable. You might even find yourself chuckling at how your ex struggled to parallel park while secretly wondering how you ever put up with their habit of eating pizza in bed. This fresh perspective can be incredibly refreshing, helping you enter future relationships with a clearer mindset.

As you dive back into the dating scene, equipped with insights from your past, remember that resilience is crucial. Dating is a series of experiments—some will work, and some will flop. Each interaction is like a new theory, and every date is an opportunity to explore your ideas about love. With every awkward dinner and failed connection, you'll sharpen your instincts and learn what truly resonates with you.

So here you are, navigating the wild landscape of love. You've faced heartbreak, shared laughs, and tackled the chaos of relationships. Now it's your turn to step confidently back into the dating world with an open heart and a renewed sense of purpose. In a universe where cats might be both alive and dead, you're learning to embrace the uncertainty of love with open arms, ready for whatever comes your way.

Ultimately, breaking up can be more about the lessons you learn rather than the loss you feel. Each experience adds a vibrant stroke to your emotional canvas, deepening your understanding of love, connection, and self-worth. So, as you prepare to move on, remember—just like Schrödinger's cat, you have the power to shape your own reality. Take

Theodore Trudeau

a deep breath, open that box, and step into a future brimming with new possibilities.

Chapter 3: Quantum Entanglement: Besties in Sync

Friends are the family we choose, and in the quirky realm of quantum physics, particles can also pick their best pals. Welcome to the fascinating world of quantum entanglement, where the connections between particles defy the usual rules about distance, time, and our everyday understanding of what friendship really means. Picture two particles, much like two best friends who can feel each other's vibes no matter how far apart they are in the universe. One could be enjoying a cosmic smoothie on a faraway planet while the other relaxes in a black hole, yet they still stay in tune with one another. This isn't just a fun image; it's the real deal, driven by the key ideas of quantum mechanics.

Think of quantum entanglement as the scientific version of a lifelong friendship. You know, that special kind where you can finish each other's sentences, anticipate their next move, or even share a telepathic bond that rivals those buddy cop duos we see on TV. Sure, we can't send a particle to grab us a coffee, but we can dive into the amazing characteristics of these entangled relationships, which show just how deep and strange their connections can be.

At its core, quantum entanglement describes what happens when two or more particles become linked together. When they are entangled, the state of one particle is instantly related to the state of another, no matter how far apart they are. This means that if one particle is spinning one way, its buddy will be spinning the opposite way, even if it's light-years away. It's as if they made a secret pact to be opposites, keeping a cosmic bond that goes against everything we think we know about space and time. Imagine it as a cosmic dance where the partners are always in sync, even when separated by mind-boggling distances.

Let's take a moment to appreciate how wild this phenomenon truly is. Picture yourself on your couch scrolling through your phone when your friend, who lives in a different state, suddenly texts you about a movie you both adore—right at the moment you were thinking about it. Spooky, right? Now, what if that connection could happen across entire galaxies instead of just states? That's quantum entanglement for you. The universe is packed with these fascinating friendships at the particle level, and it might just warm the hearts of even the most skeptical among us.

To help us grasp this concept further, let's look at the colorful side of friendship. You know how some bonds feel so deep that it seems like you're sharing thoughts? Think about those buddy comedies where two friends can't help but stumble into ridiculous situations together, as if they are held together by an invisible thread. The humor often comes from their uncanny ability to predict each other's actions, much like entangled particles that instantly respond to one another, regardless of how far apart they are.

Consider the classic sitcom "Friends," where characters like Ross and Rachel navigate their own complex entanglements—full of misunderstandings, yet always tied together by a bond that can't be broken. No way would they just move on from each other, even if one decided to jump to a different dimension. Their connection serves as a perfect analogy for quantum entanglement, where particles stay linked, sharing information in ways that seem almost magical.

The science behind this amazing connection is grounded in the principles of quantum mechanics. When particles interact, they can become entangled, meaning their properties become linked in ways that the measurement of one can instantly impact the state of the other. This isn't just a quirky theory; it's something that has been proven through experiments and is now a cornerstone of quantum physics. Studies show that when two particles are entangled, changing one particle's state leads to an immediate change in the other, no matter how far apart they are.

This instant connection has led to the phrase "spooky action at a distance," coined by none other than Albert Einstein, who was often skeptical of what entanglement meant. He saw it as something almost supernatural, like the universe was pulling strings in the background to keep these particles linked. Much like a surprising twist in a sitcom, Einstein struggled to fit this phenomenon into his understanding of the universe.

Let's also think about the practical implications of such entangled friendships. Quantum entanglement isn't just an odd idea; it has real-world uses that could change technology, communication, and even how we understand reality! Quantum computers, for example, take advantage of these entangled states to perform calculations at speeds unimaginable to regular computers. Just think about a world where we can solve problems in seconds that would take conventional computers ages!

But before we get carried away imagining a future where we all have our own quantum besties running around working for us, it's important to clarify what entanglement isn't. It doesn't allow for faster-than-light communication, nor can we send messages through these particles. It's more like an unspoken agreement between friends who can't text each other, yet seem to share a cosmic frequency. The bond is vibrant and alive, yet it operates under the rules of quantum mechanics, which can be tricky to understand, much like trying to grasp the emotional journey of your favorite sitcom character without hearing their inner thoughts.

It's no wonder that when scientists first started to explore quantum entanglement, it felt more like a plot twist from a sci-fi movie than a serious scientific study. Still, this phenomenon is as real as the cup of coffee you're sipping, and it invites us to rethink how we understand connection on both a cosmic and personal level.

As we keep exploring this delightful entanglement of particles, let's remember that these cosmic buddies are not just about scientific jargon. They prompt us to think about our own friendships—what it means to be connected, to be in sync, and to share an unbreakable bond with those we care about. Just like two entangled particles can communicate across vast distances, maybe our connections with friends and family go beyond just being close to each other.

So the next time you find yourself thinking of a friend who suddenly texts you, you might just smile and say, "Ah, we're just a couple of quantum particles in this wild universe." It's a funny thought that may not crack any scientific mysteries, but it adds a sprinkle of joy to life's intricate web of connections.

In the world of quantum physics, where particles cozy up in their entangled states, it becomes clear: friendship might just be the ultimate cosmic phenomenon, reminding us that even in the weirdest of worlds, we are all connected in mysterious and wonderful ways. So let's raise a toast to quantum besties forever—particles and people alike—because in this vast universe, it's those connections that truly make life remarkable.

Spooky Action at a Distance

In the world of physics, few phrases spark as much curiosity and confusion as "spooky action at a distance." This catchy term was coined by the brilliant Albert Einstein and sums up the puzzling idea of quantum entanglement. It pops up in discussions about particles that seem to communicate over vast distances, leaving many people puzzled. So, let's take a closer look at this phrase—not just in the cold, clinical setting of labs, but through the lens of our everyday lives, especially in the area of parental intuition.

Imagine this scene: A mother is relaxing on her couch, savoring a quiet moment after a long week of balancing work, chores, and family responsibilities. Suddenly, without warning, she feels a chill run down her spine. In an instant, she jumps up and rushes to her teenager's room, just in time to catch them climbing out the window. "What on Earth do you think you're doing?" she exclaims, her voice a mix of shock and frustration.

This uncanny ability to sense when something isn't right with their kids is often called parental intuition. It's like an instinctual radar that seems to work beyond our normal understanding. Could this maternal instinct be similar to the instant communication we see in entangled particles? It's not too far-fetched when you think about how both situations seem to break the usual rules of space and time.

    Imagine a world where every parent has an invisible link to their children, allowing them to feel when something's wrong, no matter how far apart they are. You might find this idea amusing, but let's not brush it aside entirely. After all, who hasn't had that gut feeling when something feels off with a loved one? You could be hundreds of miles away, yet something deep inside nudges you to check in. Maybe it's time we start viewing parental intuition as the quantum mechanics of family life.

    To illustrate this, picture a funny story about a mother who, even though she was a few blocks away, knew exactly when her son was trying to sneak out for a late-night adventure. The family dog, sensing something was up, barked like a neighborhood watch, alerting the mom to the mischief happening just outside her door. While scrolling through her phone, she felt an undeniable urge to peek out the window. Sure enough, there was her son, trying to pull off the sneakiest escape plan ever.

This is where the humor comes in. The kid, equipped with only a hoodie and sneakers, thought he was a master of stealth. What he didn't expect was the maternal radar that was clearly on high alert. Just like those entangled particles that instantly affect one another, this mother had a connection with her child that went beyond mere physical distance. Maybe it was a mix of instinct, love, and a sprinkle of cosmic comedy that turned this moment into something to laugh about.

But let's expand our view. The funny absurdity of these intuitive connections isn't limited to just parents and kids. Think about the bonds we share with friends. Have you ever just known when your best friend was having a tough day, even if you hadn't talked in ages? Or how about those moments when you and a close friend seem to be in sync, finishing each other's sentences or even unwittingly dressing alike for an event?

It turns out this interconnectedness—similar to how entangled particles behave—might actually have a quantum foundation that supports the idea of non-local connections in our lives. While friends aren't communicating through quantum means, there's something wonderfully amusing about how our relationships echo the principles that govern the universe.

To dig a bit deeper, let's take a playful look at quantum entanglement itself. When two particles become entangled, they form a bond that ties their states together, meaning that measuring one instantly influences the state of the other. Imagine it as a cosmic game of tag, where the two players are forever linked, regardless of the distance they might travel in the quantum playground. The way these particles interact seems almost magical.

Now, you might be curious about how this quirky science connects to our daily lives. The humor in quantum mechanics often arises when scientists try to wrap their heads around the implications of entanglement in the real world. For example, researchers are looking into how entangled particles could lead to advances in quantum communication and computing. This could change how we share information, creating secure communication that's nearly impossible to intercept.

Picture a future where your texts are sent with the kind of security that would make even a CIA agent envious, all thanks to the antics of those rambunctious entangled particles. You send a message to a friend, and instantly, the information zips through these quantum connections, making eavesdropping feel like trying to eavesdrop on a conversation happening in another dimension. Sounds like something out of a sci-fi movie, doesn't it? Yet, the possibilities are both thrilling and wonderfully absurd.

Bringing it back to our everyday lives, we can't overlook the humor in how often our intuitive connections seem to reflect the strange behavior of particles. Imagine a group of friends gathered for a movie night with plenty of snacks. As the hours go by, it becomes clear that their minds are connected in a bizarre way. Someone suggests pizza, and before they finish, another friend chimes in with the exact toppings they were just about to mention. The synchronicity is so uncanny that you can't help but chuckle, wondering if they've stumbled into a world where their thoughts are entangled, just like particles in the quantum realm.

And it doesn't stop there. The cosmic comedy continues when we find ourselves in situations where our intuitive connections take the lead. Have you ever been with friends and suddenly burst into laughter, only to discover that everyone was thinking the same joke? It's as though a cosmic thread binds the room, weaving shared humor into a collective experience that goes beyond normal conversation.

However, we should be careful. While it's fun to enjoy the playful similarities between quantum entanglement and our intuitive relationships, there are practical limits to keep in mind. Entangled particles follow the rules of quantum mechanics, which means they can't be used for faster-than-light communication. So, while you may feel an urge to reach out to a friend in crisis, it doesn't mean you can send them a telepathic message.

Still, there's a delightful silliness in how we navigate these connections. Just as quantum entanglement pushes the boundaries of distance and communication, our intuition challenges our views on connection and empathy in our everyday lives.

Every day gives us countless chances to marvel at the quirks of our connections. Whether it's a text that arrives at just the right moment or an unexpected encounter with a friend, we can feel those cosmic threads weaving through our lives. We become part of a larger story that reflects the strange yet beautiful nature of existence.

So, the next time you share a knowing look with a friend or sense that your child is up to something, take a moment to appreciate the humor and wonder in your relationships. You might just be tapping into a cosmic connection that rivals the intricate dance of entangled particles in the universe.

The interplay between "spooky action at a distance" and our everyday experiences reminds us that life is full of delightful mysteries waiting to be explored. Whether we look at it through the lens of quantum mechanics or the amusing quirks of our own intuitive connections, there's a kind of magic in how we relate to one another. As we journey together through this crazy adventure, let's remember to celebrate the joy and laughter that come from the complexities of our interconnected lives, all while pondering the strange and wonderful science that shapes our universe. In this grand cosmic picture, where particles are like best friends and parents have a knack for sensing trouble, we find inspiration to embrace the delightful absurdities that fill our relationships.

Teleportation Dreams

Imagine a world where commuting is just a thing of the past, like a faded memory of when people spent hours stuck in traffic or wedged into crowded buses and trains. In this amazing place, when you crave a cup of coffee, you don't have to make a long drive to your go-to café. Instead, you simply picture that hot cup of coffee, and before you even finish your mental order, you find yourself standing at the counter, the barista flashing a knowing smile as he hands you a perfectly brewed cappuccino. Welcome to the fantasy of teleportation, where the ordinary becomes extraordinary and our daily lives get an exciting upgrade.

Now, before you start imagining flashy sci-fi spaceships or wild gadgets that look like a mix between a blender and a time machine, let's clear things up. The teleportation we're talking about isn't about whisking you off to a faraway galaxy or pulling you from your cozy couch and dropping you in a busy café in Paris. No, this kind of teleportation is rooted in the fascinating world of quantum physics, specifically the phenomenon known as quantum teleportation. But don't let that sound too complicated; we're not going to get too deep into the science without having a little fun.

Quantum teleportation is a stunning idea that involves sending information instantly, especially the states of particles, rather than physically moving objects. Think of it like sending a text message across the universe, where your phone doesn't actually travel but rather sends the information it holds. Picture that moment of excitement when you hit "send" on a message, and in the blink of an eye, it zooms off to your friend miles away. The phone didn't go anywhere; it was just the information that covered the distance. Now, imagine taking that image and applying it to the idea of teleporting yourself to that coffee shop—only instead of moving your whole body through space, you're sending your very essence to the spot you want to be.

To make this more relatable, let's think about your typical Tuesday morning. You wake up, groggy and craving your first sip of caffeine. You dream of the perfect coffee—smooth, aromatic, and just sweet enough. You could go through the hassle of putting on clothes and driving to your local café, or you could just close your eyes and *teleport* there. Boom! You find yourself in front of the barista, your order already in the system thanks to a quantum transfer of your thoughts directly to the café's register. "One cappuccino, extra foam, please," you say, and just like that, your drink is ready and waiting. No lines, no waiting—just pure bliss served in a ceramic cup.

Now, let's take a moment to think about the funny situations that could happen if teleportation were real. Picture this: instead of arriving at work all flustered after a long commute, you could just teleport straight into your office, coffee in hand, looking fresh and ready for the day. Your coworkers would stare in amazement, wondering if you were some sort of wizard or if you'd discovered a new level of productivity. The office would turn into a place of endless possibilities, where water cooler chatter could be filled with teleportation mishaps. "Did you hear about Steve? He tried to teleport for a quick meeting but ended up in the break room with all the donuts!" Just think of the laughter those lighthearted moments would bring, where teleportation could spark a whole new kind of office humor.

And let's not forget the funny implications for social events. Imagine your friend's wedding, set in a sprawling location that's tough for most to reach. But why bother with the hassle of travel? You could just teleport right into the middle of the ceremony, arriving perfectly on time with not a hair out of place. You'd be able to pop into parties, feel the vibe instantly, and know exactly when to make your grand entrance. "Oh, they're out of cake? Time to teleport back home and grab a slice from the fridge!" You could become the life of the party, making spontaneous comebacks and never missing out on the fun.

But let's not ignore the everyday annoyances teleportation could erase. Think about grocery shopping. No more endless aisles packed with indecisive shoppers or waiting behind someone who insists on using coupons for every single item. Instead, you could teleport straight to the produce section, grab an avocado, and zip back home before you even notice you've left your couch. Of course, the grocery store would have to keep track of all these teleporting shoppers. "Hey, why did you just teleport in and out in less than a minute? That's suspicious!" The store manager might need to hire teleportation monitors to make sure no one is taking advantage of the system.

This fun vision of teleportation also raises some amusing questions: what if our teleportation tech came with its own quirks? Imagine accidentally miscalculating your destination and ending up in your boss's office instead of your favorite café. "Um... I meant to teleport to the coffee shop," you might stutter, trying to explain your unexpected arrival. Or think of an excited friend who joyfully teleports to your backyard for a surprise visit, only to land hilariously in your inflatable pool. The laughter that would follow as they splash around in disbelief could kick off a new trend: "The teleportation pool party! Bring your swimsuit!"

Now, let's take a closer look at the science behind this teleportation dream. At the core of quantum teleportation is the idea of entangled particles. When particles become entangled, they create a strange connection that allows them to share information instantly, no matter how far apart they are. It's like they have a secret handshake that goes beyond the physical space between them. Imagine two best friends who, even though they live in different places, can finish each other's sentences—that's basically quantum entanglement at work.

When one particle's quantum state is measured, its entangled partner instantly changes, almost as if they're having a chat in a unique language only they understand. This mysterious link allows quantum teleportation to happen. Essentially, the information about one particle's state can be sent to another spot, letting it be recreated there without the particle itself ever needing to travel. It's like playing the ultimate game of charades, where one particle is the player in one location, and the other particle guesses the move, even from miles away.

You might be thinking, "That sounds great, but what about me? I want to teleport!" Well, while quantum teleportation is a real thing happening at the level of tiny particles, using it in our everyday lives is still a long way off. Scientists are making progress, but for now, the idea of teleporting ourselves remains firmly in the realm of science fiction. Yet, just dreaming about it is exciting, isn't it? The thrilling idea of a future where we can travel instantly, breaking free from the limits of time and space.

Let's take a moment to think about the frustrations of commuting and how they inspire us to dream of teleportation. Commuting often feels like a black hole, swallowing up hours we could spend doing things we truly enjoy. We've all felt that moment of despair when we're stuck in traffic, watching the seconds crawl by, our patience wearing thinner than a thread. The idea of teleportation is like a light at the end of that tunnel, a bright glimpse of a world where we can escape the grind of our vehicles and confidently step into our desired destinations without the hassle.

But even as we fantasize about teleportation, let's not overlook the humor in our current travel experiences. Travel memes are everywhere, poking fun at the ridiculousness of long airport lines, cramped airplane seats, and the never-ending struggle for overhead bin space. The contrast between these everyday headaches and the dream of teleportation highlights our shared desire for instant travel—an escape from the ordinary that brings a smile as we chuckle at the absurdity of our daily routines.

While we imagine a world where teleportation is as common as checking the weather, we can also think about how it would change our social interactions. Would we take our friendships for granted? If you could teleport to see your friends anytime, would you still plan hangouts? Or would those spontaneous visits turn into a new way of connecting, where popping in unannounced became normal? Just like in our imagined teleportation future, those little surprises could lead to laughter and connection in ways we've never considered.

In the end, the idea of teleportation not only gives us a peek into a fascinating world shaped by the rules of quantum mechanics but also offers a treasure trove of laughter and relatable moments. The potential for instant travel may still be a dream waiting to be explored, but it ignites our imagination and lets us envision a world beyond the limits of space and time. So, as you sip your coffee and daydream about teleportation possibilities, remember the joy and giggles that come from imagining a life where commuting is a thing of the past and spontaneity is king. The universe is vast, filled with wonders waiting to be discovered, and who knows? Maybe someday we'll step boldly into the unknown, ready to embrace the whimsical adventure of teleportation. Until then, let's keep finding joy in our daily lives, knowing that quantum mechanics reflects the delightful connections we share.

Theodore Trudeau

Chapter 4: Heisenberg's Uncertainty Principle: Everyday Mysteries

Have you ever had that sinking feeling when you realize your phone is missing? You know the drill: one minute you're happily scrolling through your social media, and the next you're tearing apart your house looking for it. You start with the couch cushions, digging through a mystery mix of crumbs and that random receipt from three months ago. You glance under the couch, which seems to be a black hole for everything that needs to be found. You check your pockets, the table, the bathroom, and even that junk drawer filled with odds and ends you never know what to do with.

If you're anything like me, your heart races as you try to remember the last time you actually saw it. Suddenly, the outside world fades away, and you find yourself retracing your steps like a detective in a movie, where the crime is your own absent-mindedness. Is your phone even real, or have you accidentally wandered into some alternate reality where cell phones don't exist? The pressure builds with every unsuccessful search. It's during these moments that I can't help but think of the Heisenberg Uncertainty Principle.

This principle tells us that certain pairs of properties, like position and momentum, can't be measured at the same time with complete accuracy. The more you focus on one, the less clear the other becomes. So, while you're on the hunt for your phone, you're caught in this chaotic swirl of uncertainty. Every time you think you've pinpointed its location, a nagging thought creeps in: what if it slipped off the counter as you juggled your coffee? Or what if it fell out of your pocket when you rushed to catch the bus?

Isn't that just like life? A series of uncertain moments where the only certainty is that we're bound to misplace our phones when we need them the most. Losing your phone isn't just annoying; it perfectly captures life's unpredictability, where outcomes are never guaranteed and surprises pop up when you least expect them.

Let's take a step back for a moment. When you finally find your phone—because let's face it, it's usually in some totally ordinary place like the kitchen counter or buried under a pile of laundry—you feel a rush of excitement. It's that "aha!" moment, kind of like finally getting that Schrödinger's cat experiment isn't really about a cat in a box facing some existential crisis, but rather what happens when we don't observe things.

In the world of quantum mechanics, particles exist in a state of possibility; they are both here and not here until we take a look. Similarly, when we misplace our phones, they float in this limbo state, switching between being lost and found until we finally spot them. Our phones become like tiny quantum particles, wandering through the corners of our homes, hiding right next to those socks that vanished from the laundry.

The ridiculousness of searching for that elusive phone shows just how much our daily lives mirror quantum principles. We navigate through uncertainty with every single decision we make, whether it's picking out our clothes or deciding what to have for dinner, creating an endless loop of choices and consequences.

Now, think about how this principle plays out in everyday decisions. Picture this: it's dinner time, and you're scrolling through options on your favorite food delivery app. Every choice brings a fresh wave of uncertainty. How spicy is that curry? Will the tacos be fresh? What if I order sushi and get food poisoning? Just like those particles in the quantum world, deciding what to eat can feel complicated, with the perfect outcome slipping away like a quantum state. The more you fixate on one option, like the spiciness of the curry, the less sure you become about the others.

This uncertainty is a delicate dance, a reflection of the quantum nature of life. It's a nod to the chaos we create with each decision we face. Sometimes we feel frozen, stuck between choices, like an electron spinning in its orbit, unsure of where it is or what it's doing.

Consider how this uncertainty plays out when we're faced with choices. Have you ever stood in front of your closet, overwhelmed by all the outfit possibilities? You might find yourself stuck between two shirts, anxiously trying to figure out which will earn more compliments or make you feel the most confident. Just like measuring the position and momentum of a particle, every choice has its consequences that ripple through your day.

Just as particles behave differently based on observation, our own choices lead us to unexpected consequences. Sometimes you wear that bold red dress, and it's the best decision ever—everyone notices you, and you feel incredible. Other times, you opt for something comfy but questionable, only to find that comfort doesn't always equal style.

In the realm of quantum mechanics, we are all explorers, seeking to understand the chaotic dance of possibilities that shape our lives. Just as physicists run experiments to better grasp how particles behave, we experiment with the flow of our daily choices. What shirt should I wear? What should I eat for dinner? How often will I check my phone today? These questions may seem small, but they capture the essence of uncertainty that surrounds us.

Embracing uncertainty can be exciting. It encourages us to approach life with curiosity, allowing us to enjoy the unexpected twists that come our way. Maybe you'll discover a new favorite dish you never thought to try. Perhaps you'll meet a new friend at the grocery store who opens your eyes to a different perspective. Like those quantum particles, our lives are shaped by unpredictability, and that uncertainty is what makes life truly interesting.

So, the next time you misplace your phone, take a moment to think about the chaos around you. Remember, you're not just on a quest for a device; you're navigating the unpredictable maze of life, much like scientists trying to understand how particles behave. Embrace the excitement of uncertainty!

Ironically, you might find that the search—complete with all its misadventures and moments of panic—leads you to something even more valuable than your phone: a deeper appreciation for life's delightful chaos.

And who knows? That phone of yours might just be hiding in plain sight, reminding you that sometimes, amidst all the uncertainty, what you're looking for is closer than you think.

Uncertainty in Everyday Life

Imagine this: it's a Thursday evening, and you're standing in front of your refrigerator, feeling totally stuck. You've got a half-empty jar of mustard, a mysterious container of leftovers that seems like it might have a life of its own, and a few sad-looking vegetables that could be okay. Choosing what to have for dinner turns into an inner debate that feels almost as complicated as a United Nations meeting. On one hand, a quick peanut butter and jelly sandwich sounds comforting and easy. On the other hand, you can't shake your craving for that delicious gourmet stir-fry you had at that trendy new restaurant last week—the one with waitstaff sporting ironic mustaches and a menu written on a surfboard.

But here's the problem: you're stuck. The more you think about your options, the more you feel like a deer caught in the headlights. What if I mess up the stir-fry? What if the mustard is actually expired? And then there's that voice in your head asking, "You had toast for breakfast, are you really going to have PB&J again?" It's a classic case of indecision, where every choice feels like a potential mistake waiting to happen. The uncertainty of what to eat almost mirrors the strange behavior of particles in the quantum world.

Let's take a moment to explore how this chaotic dinner decision-making is similar to the principles of quantum mechanics. Heisenberg's Uncertainty Principle tells us that you can't measure certain pairs of properties, like position and momentum, at the same time with absolute accuracy. The more you focus on one, the less clear the other becomes. In your dinner scenario, the more you dream about the stir-fry being a culinary hit, the less you pay attention to the mustard's quirky appeal. Soon, both options start to feel like fuzzy blurbs in your mind.

Now, let's introduce a friend who knows this struggle all too well. We'll call him Dan. He's the type of guy who takes what feels like forever to choose a restaurant. You're standing in a parking lot, your stomach growling, while Dan weighs the pros and cons of the Thai place versus that new taco truck. "I heard great things about their pad Thai," he thinks out loud, "but I really want some tacos too. Tacos are always a safe bet, right?" You can practically see the wheels turning in his mind, each option becoming more complicated as he overanalyzes every possible outcome.

Dan's dilemma isn't just about food; it reflects something deeper about the human experience. He's a living example of quantum uncertainty in action. Just like particles that change when we watch them, our choices can shift based on how we view them. The moment Dan decides he wants tacos, another part of him worries he might regret missing out on that tasty pad Thai.

After what feels like an eternity, Dan finally makes a choice—he orders tacos. But as you both dig in, he can't help but say, "What if I should've gotten pad Thai? Maybe next time." This, my friend, is what we all go through: we make choices while constantly wondering about the other options we left behind. It's a cycle of second-guessing that can keep us spinning for ages, much like how particles jump between states.

So, why do we get so tangled up in uncertainty? Maybe it's the fear of making wrong choices. How often do we overthink the little things? Will the shoes I pick match my outfit? What if I order a drink that tastes bad? Is my salad dressing too tangy? Each question nudges us further into a maze of doubt.

Now, let's switch gears to another situation you might relate to. Imagine you've just received a job offer. At first glance, it seems fantastic—better pay, a more impressive title, and the chance to work with a highly regarded team. But then the doubts start creeping in. Is this really the right move for you? What if you leave behind friends you've made? What if you end up disliking the new office culture? Suddenly, uncertainties are piling up, like a wave of questions crashing over you.

Here's the twist: as you think things through, you find yourself bouncing between excitement and anxiety, much like an electron caught in a quantum state. The more you try to pin down your feelings about the new job, the hazier they become. You might daydream about your future—envisioning the office, your potential coworkers, and the opportunities for growth—only to be yanked back to reality by worries about what you might lose.

Just like Dan's dinner dilemma, accepting change calls for us to step into the unknown, to face the uncertainties that make life both thrilling and scary. Eventually, you have to take a chance, knowing that every decision comes with its share of unknowns. Sometimes, just like those unpredictable quantum particles, the results can surprise you in ways you never saw coming.

Think back to a time when you took a chance on something uncertain—perhaps traveling solo to a new country or attending an event where you didn't know anyone. Each of those moments was filled with uncertainty, yet they often led to the most incredible experiences. You return with stories that could fill a book, friendships that stretch across the globe, and maybe even a newfound confidence in navigating life's unpredictability.

The small choices we make each day, from what to wear to how we spend our weekends, shape our lives in profound ways. They are the building blocks of our routines, yet they also offer chances to embrace the full complexity of life. Each time you lean into uncertainty, you're participating in your own little experiment—a dance of possibilities, waiting to see how it all turns out.

Perhaps that's the key to living a fulfilling life: realizing that uncertainty isn't your enemy. It's woven into the fabric of existence. When you embrace uncertainty, you open yourself up to the excitement of the unknown—the anticipation of what's to come, and the chance for unexpected surprises. After all, life is more like a buffet of opportunities rather than a fixed menu. You'll never know if that curry will delight your palate or set it ablaze until you take that first bite.

So, next time you're faced with a decision—whether it's what to whip up for dinner, whether to take that new job, or which book to read—think of Dan. Remember the indecision, and recognize that life is all about navigating the unpredictable. Allow yourself to take risks, explore the unknown, and embrace the wonderful uncertainties that make life so rich and vibrant.

As you reflect on your next choice, keep in mind that every decision—big or small—adds to the beautiful chaos of life. And who knows? You might discover something delightful along the way that adds a surprising twist to your journey. So go ahead, take that leap, order those tacos, or say yes to that new job. After all, the true flavor of life often comes from welcoming the uncertainty we encounter in our everyday experiences.

Indecision: Particles and People

Picture this: you're settled in front of your favorite streaming service, remote in hand, while the world outside buzzes with life. The wind rustles the trees, and the sun begins to dip below the horizon, casting a cozy glow in your living room. But there you sit, frozen by the endless options in front of you. Should you dive into that new action movie everyone's raving about? Or maybe you'd prefer a heartfelt indie film that promises to tug at your heartstrings? The catch is, you can't seem to make a decision. It's a classic moment of indecision that feels all too familiar, like a bad case of déjà vu.

This situation mirrors the fascinating world of quantum mechanics, particularly the idea of wave-particle duality. At its core, particles like electrons can exist in multiple states at the same time until they're measured. They're a lot like those flickering movie options in front of you—until you pick one, they linger in a state of possibility. Just like a photon that can act like both a wave and a particle, your choice hangs in the air of uncertainty, waiting for a little push to one side or the other.

Think back to those frantic nights of choosing a movie. You scroll through the titles, and with each click, the potential outcomes shift like sand beneath your feet. You finally settle on a gripping thriller, but as the credits roll, a nagging thought creeps in: "What if that rom-com would have been a better pick?" The moment you hit play, all the other choices vanish into one reality, echoing the quantum principle that once you measure a particle's position, its wave function collapses into a clear state. When it comes to decision-making, weighing the potential outcomes is just like committing to a choice.

Let's meet Sophie, a friend who often finds herself in this classic movie-picking dilemma. Sophie approaches her movie choices like a scientist prepping for an experiment. She starts with thorough research, scanning reviews, checking ratings, and even watching trailers. The pressure feels intense—what if the movie is awful, and she ends up wasting precious hours? The weight of her indecision grows, making her realize that she's missing out on the simple joy of just watching something.

This struggle isn't limited to movies; it spills over into other parts of her life. Recently, Sophie faced the tough decision between two job offers. One promised stability and a steady routine, while the other held the thrill of adventure and the chance to explore new horizons in her career. For weeks, she wavered between the two, gripped by the fear of making the wrong choice. Friends and family weighed in, and with each conversation, the uncertainty only deepened. Just like particles in a quantum state, her possible paths stayed undefined until she made a decisive move.

One evening, Sophie decided to tackle her indecision in a fun way. She came up with a game to break the cycle: she wrote down each movie or job option on slips of paper and tossed them into a jar. With a mix of excitement and anxiety, she drew a slip, hoping it would bring her clarity. But here's the twist: the moment she picked one slip, the other option began to call to her, whispering sweet nothings about the adventure she just passed up. It was a classic case of indecision; her mind had settled on one choice, yet the echoes of uncertainty lingered.

This dance of indecision is one we can all relate to. We often find ourselves caught in a state of potential, wrestling with choices that feel equally exciting and equally scary. Much like particles in quantum mechanics, we can flit between possibilities, each one holding a different potential outcome. This is especially true in life-changing moments—whether considering a partner, moving to a new city, or picking the perfect book to read on a rainy day.

Taking a step back, we can see the absurdity in our indecision. Sometimes, we toggle between two options that ultimately lead to similar outcomes, just like a particle that exists in a superposition. Imagine standing in front of a bakery, torn between a croissant and a danish. The moment you finally make your choice, the other pastry seems to taunt you from the display case, as if it knew all along that you'd pick the croissant. It's a tasty dilemma that echoes that quantum quandary—once you select a pastry, the other slips away into the realm of "what could have been."

As we explore indecision, we can't ignore the humor and depth in those moments when we think we know what we want, only to be thrown off by unexpected twists. Picture the classic scenario of arriving at your favorite restaurant, only to find that the dish you were eagerly anticipating has just been taken off the menu. Suddenly, you're left scrambling to reassess your options, much like electrons swirling around an atom, their paths unpredictable and ever-changing. In those moments, making a decision feels like navigating the uncertain waters of quantum physics.

Anecdotes abound, perfectly illustrating the delicate balance between potential and commitment. Take a friend who spent ages debating which vacation spot would be her dream getaway. The more she researched, the more overwhelming her choices became. Should she soak in the sun on the beaches of Mexico or wander through the charming streets of a quaint European town? She created spreadsheets, sought advice from travel blogs, and even consulted her astrological sign for guidance. Yet, every choice felt tempting, and every minute spent in indecision felt like another wave crashing against her shore of excitement.

In the end, she opted for a spontaneous beach trip, where she enjoyed a delightful mix of sun, sand, and perhaps a few too many piña coladas. Yet during her vacation, she couldn't shake thoughts of those captivating European streets. It was as if quantum particles were toggling between states, reminding her that every choice is a leap into the unknown, filled with both beauty and uncertainty.

These reflections guide us to a deeper understanding: indecision isn't a flaw; it's a part of being human. It shows that we're considering the complexity of the world and weighing our options against a backdrop of endless possibilities. It's easy to see indecision as a foe, a burden we need to shake off. But what if we shifted our view? What if we welcomed our uncertainty with humor and openness, recognizing that some of life's greatest joys lie just beyond that initial leap of faith?

As we share our experiences, it's clear that indecision isn't a permanent state. It's a dance—a lively tango of potential and reality, of choices made and opportunities missed. Every decision you make shapes the path of your life, much like the unpredictable nature of quantum particles. Your choices create ripples that can lead to delightful surprises you never saw coming. So, the next time you find yourself stuck in indecision, remember that you're not alone. You're part of the cosmic dance of existence, where each step brings you closer to new experiences and unexpected outcomes.

By embracing uncertainty, we can cultivate a lighter, more playful attitude toward decision-making. Instead of facing choices with dread, see them as chances for discovery. Give yourself the freedom to explore possibilities, experiment with different paths, and recognize that every decision can lead to growth—whether it brings a delightful surprise or an unexpected lesson.

As we wrap up this exploration, let's remember that, much like quantum mechanics, life is filled with complex, unpredictable interactions. The choices we face may feel daunting, yet they also unveil a rich landscape full of discovery. Embrace the unknown with an open heart; let the fluid nature of your decisions reflect the dance of particles in the universe. Each choice you make, just like a wave collapsing into a particle, opens up new realities that paint the canvas of your life.

Take a moment to consider your next decision—be it something as simple as dinner or a major life change. Think of it as an experiment in the grand laboratory of life. Allow yourself to ride the waves of uncertainty with curiosity and joy. Just as particles exist in a dance of possibility, our choices swim in a vibrant sea of potential. Embrace the journey of decision-making, for it's within that journey that the true beauty of life unfolds.

Theodore Trudeau

Chapter 5: Quantum Tunneling: Sneaking Past Life's Obstacles

Imagine this: You're at a lively party, surrounded by friends, acquaintances, and maybe even that one person who always gets a bit too excited about karaoke. The music is pumping, laughter bounces off the walls, and there's an unmistakable buzz in the air. You start to feel a bit hungry, and your eyes are locked onto that glorious snack table sitting enticingly on the other side of the room. But oh no! There's a bustling crowd standing between you and those tasty chips and dip.

Now, if we think about this the traditional way, you might picture yourself pushing through the throng. You'd have to weave around people, squeezing past two friends deep in a ten-minute debate about the meaning of cat videos online. It sounds like a tough job, and let's be honest, not the most fun way to get a snack.

But what if, just for a moment, we tossed out the usual rules of physics? What if you could simply *pop* over to the snack table without having to deal with the crowd at all? You'd be like a magic particle, doing something that would astonish everyone around you. It sounds a bit like a fantasy, doesn't it? This playful idea of slipping through barriers—be they the physical ones of a crowded room or the metaphorical ones in our lives—is exactly what quantum tunneling is about.

At its heart, quantum tunneling is all about how particles can move through barriers that, according to traditional physics, they just shouldn't be able to pass. Imagine a tiny electron facing a solid wall. Classical physics would say that the electron needs enough energy to climb over that wall. But in the quantum world, things get a little weird. This little electron has a clever trick. Instead of needing to work hard to climb over the wall, it can simply phase through it, as if the wall were made of thin air.

Let's break it down a bit more. In the quantum universe, particles exist in a state of uncertainty instead of certainty. They're like that friend who can't decide whether to go out or stay in with their favorite show. Because of this uncertainty, particles can be on either side of a barrier at any moment. They might be here, they might be there, or they could even be in both places at once—like that one friend who swears they can make it to dinner and still hang out at the bar.

To help visualize this, let's call in our furry friend, the cat. Not just any cat, but a meme-worthy feline that perfectly captures Heisenberg's uncertainty principle. Picture this cat standing in front of a door, fluffy and confused. In the realm of quantum mechanics, the door doesn't represent a solid barrier. Instead, it's more like a suggestion. With a sprinkle of quantum magic, this cat can occupy both sides of the door frame at the same time, peeking through as if solidity is just a pesky illusion.

It's this odd duality that makes quantum tunneling not only a cool scientific idea but also something we can relate to in our everyday lives. Much like when we procrastinate, we often find ourselves avoiding tasks that loom over us, like a barrier that feels impossible to cross. Whether it's tackling a messy house, responding to that email you've been dodging, or facing that mountain of laundry, we sometimes find ways to sneak past our own obstacles just like a particle slipping through a wall.

Think about it for a second. Have you ever stared down a daunting task, only to put it off so well that suddenly the deadline is looming? You know the drill: the clock is ticking, the pressure is on, but somehow you manage to "tunnel" through the challenge at the last minute, scrambling to get everything done in a caffeine-fueled frenzy.

Now, quantum tunneling isn't just for electrons and particles. It has big implications across different scientific fields, including chemistry, electronics, and even how our universe works. Take nuclear fusion, for example. It's the tunneling process that allows light atomic nuclei to push past their natural repulsion and fuse together, creating energy that powers our stars—including the sun that lights up Earth. Without this fascinating phenomenon, the universe as we know it would be a whole lot different.

Let's not forget the humorous side of this! Picture a world where everything worked on the principles of quantum tunneling. You could be at your desk, pretending to focus, while in reality, you've ventured into the land of YouTube cat videos without even leaving your chair. Your boss might scratch their head, wondering how you vanished into thin air, while you snack on metaphorical chips and dip in your procrastination paradise. It's a funny image, and it shows how quantum mechanics can reflect our daily lives in amusing, unexpected ways.

Overall, quantum tunneling reminds us that boundaries—whether they are physical, mental, or societal—are often more flexible than we realize. Just as particles can slip through barriers, we too can find ways to navigate life's hurdles. Approach them with a bit of creativity and some humor, and you might discover that you can wiggle past challenges that once felt overwhelming.

So next time you find yourself at a crowded gathering, remember this: you're not just another partygoer; you're a quantum particle in a world filled with endless possibilities. With a splash of imagination and maybe a dash of humor, you can dance your way through life's obstacles while enjoying the snack table of existence.

Overcoming Obstacles: Tunneling Through Life's Challenges

Life can sometimes feel like a vast, twisting maze, filled with challenges that seem impossible to overcome. You might look at your to-do list and feel like you're staring up at a mountain. Anxiety can settle in as you wonder how you'll ever get through it all. We've all been there, caught up in the chaos of daily life, dodging responsibilities like we're in a game of dodgeball where the balls are deadlines and societal pressures. But what if, instead of giving in to that pressure, we found a way to navigate through these challenges?

Let's start with something we can all relate to: public speaking. If there's one fear that ranks high on everyone's list, it's talking in front of a crowd, right up there with spiders and heights. Picture this: you're standing in front of a group, your hands are sweating like you just ran a marathon in a sauna. The words you want to say feel jumbled in your mind, swirling together like a tornado, and you can't help but notice that one person in the front row who looks like they'd rather be watching paint dry.

But don't panic! You have an unexpected ally at your disposal—humor. Imagine you're up there, feeling the tension, but instead of freezing up, you crack a self-deprecating joke about how you'd rather be chatting with your cat about the stock market (who, let's be honest, is the only one who truly gets your investment strategy). Suddenly, the room erupts with laughter, and the atmosphere shifts from tense to lighthearted. You've not only broken through that intimidating fear but also created a connection that turns what could have been an awkward moment into a fun and memorable experience.

In those moments, you've done a little magic of your own. You've found a way to push through the heavy wall of anxiety with a clever twist: realizing that laughter is a universal language that can ease even the toughest situations. Life often throws us into the deep end, but just like a particle squeezing through an energy barrier, we can navigate our way through. Humor can be the spark that helps us leap over obstacles we once thought were impossible.

Now, let's switch gears and talk about job interviews. Ah, the ultimate challenge of the corporate world. You walk in, clutching your resume like it's a life vest. The room feels thick with tension, and the interviewer looks at you as if they're trying to figure out a challenging puzzle—only they seem more interested in your choices than the job itself. Every question feels like a trap, ready to swallow you up if you step on the wrong answer. Your heart races, your palms start to sweat, and for a split second, you think about bolting out the door.

But hold on! What if, instead of seeing this as a wall you have to conquer, you flipped your perspective? You're not just a job candidate; you're an adventurous traveler seeking a new experience. You sit up a little taller, smile, and approach the interview like a friendly chat over coffee. As the questions come, you share stories from your past—like the time you accidentally spilled coffee on your boss, but it turned into a bonding moment over messy mishaps. Suddenly, that towering wall feels more like a small bump, and you're breezing right over it.

This shift in thinking can change everything. Just like a particle figuring out how to navigate around a barrier, you can tackle the tricky world of job interviews by rethinking the situation to ease your worries. By embracing your quirks and humor, you can tell a story that highlights your skills and lets your personality shine.

Now, let's talk about something many of us face: dating. If navigating the dating world isn't a true test of your ability to break through barriers, I don't know what is. First dates are often packed with expectations, nerves, and that awkward feeling of sitting across from someone, both of you realizing you chose to be here at the same time—it's like a cosmic coincidence. You might find yourself trying not to spill your drink while steering clear of touchy subjects like politics, religion, and your childhood obsession with collecting Beanie Babies.

But here's where the real magic happens. Instead of letting the fear of awkward silence hold you back, lean into the discomfort with humor. Share a funny story about one of your most embarrassing moments—like the time you tried to impress someone by cooking a fancy dinner and ended up setting off the smoke alarm, leading to a visit from the fire department. Sure, it might feel like you've just dug a tunnel straight into your most embarrassing memories, but by showing your vulnerable side, you build a genuine connection that goes beyond the initial awkwardness.

Think about it: often, the barriers we feel in dating (and in life) are ones we create ourselves. When we allow ourselves to be relatable and human, we unlock doors to deeper connections—just like particles finding their way through barriers that look impossible to cross. So next time you feel nervous about a first date, remember that it's okay to be a little goofy, a little vulnerable, and totally real. The best connections usually happen when we dare to tunnel past our fears and step into the light of authenticity.

Speaking of authenticity, let's take a moment to appreciate how our friends can amplify these tunneling experiences. Imagine you're preparing for a big presentation at work, feeling like you're auditioning for the role of "Nervous Wreck" in a soap opera. You're pacing back and forth, rehearsing your lines, and anxiety is creeping in like an uninvited guest.

Just when you think you're about to spiral into panic, your phone buzzes. It's your best friend sending you a hilarious meme of a cat in a tie, furiously typing at a laptop. The caption reads, "When you're trying to look professional but you're really just winging it." In an instant, the tension lifts. You chuckle, and suddenly the walls feel a bit less daunting.

This is the magic of friendship—sometimes, all it takes is one light-hearted moment to help us push through our worries. Friends can turn obstacles into chances for laughter and connection. They remind us that life doesn't always have to be serious and that humor can brighten even the most challenging situations.

These shared experiences remind us that we're not alone in our struggles. Everyone faces obstacles that once felt too big to handle. Whether it's the fear of public speaking, the pressure of an interview, or the uncertainty of dating, we all encounter moments that make us want to retreat. Yet, just like particles in the quantum realm, we have a remarkable ability to slip through barriers and come out stronger, often with a newfound sense of humor.

As we navigate the ups and downs of our lives, remember that we can change how we view obstacles. We can choose to see challenges as chances for growth, laughter, and connection. By embracing our quirks and letting humor guide us, we can find our way through the barriers life throws at us.

So the next time you face a challenge, big or small, channel your inner quantum particle. Laugh at your stumbles, lean on your friends for support, and remember that sometimes, a little creativity is all it takes to get past the obstacles in your way. With a touch of humor and a sprinkle of imagination, those solid walls may turn out to be nothing more than illusions, waiting to be navigated in this wonderfully unpredictable adventure we call life.

Mario Kart's Rainbow Road Parallel: Navigating Chaos

Imagine this: you're speeding down a colorful track, with a catchy tune playing in the background. It's a bright, sunny day in the Mushroom Kingdom, and you're in the middle of an intense race on Rainbow Road, the most wild and colorful track ever created. Your heart is racing, your fingers are gripping the controller, and you can feel the thrill in your stomach. Victory seems so close! But hold on—a banana peel lies right in your way! You try to dodge it, but your timing is off. In an instant, you're flying off the edge, watching your dreams of winning disappear into the vast abyss below.

Ah, Rainbow Road, where everything feels intense and chaotic. Life often mirrors this exhilarating race, filled with surprising twists, turns, and hurdles that can throw us off our game at any time. Just like the unpredictable nature of this iconic Mario Kart track, life can have us soaring to new heights one moment, and crashing down the next. It's a whimsical yet wild dance, requiring skill, strategy, and a sense of humor to navigate effectively.

The Idiot's Guide to Quantum Physics

As you zoom around Rainbow Road, every curve can feel like a jump into the unknown. You hold onto the controller tightly, prepared for whatever surprises might come your way. One minute, you're smoothly gliding along a rainbow-colored path, and the next, you're avoiding shells, banana peels, and the dreaded "Blue Shell" lurking around the corner. Those moments when you're airborne and feeling on top of the world are electrifying. They represent the small wins in life when everything seems to fall perfectly into place. But let's not forget the perilous edges that can send you spiraling into nothingness.

These chaotic experiences serve as a relatable reflection of quantum tunneling. In the quantum world, particles can defy the odds, slipping through barriers that seem impossible to cross. It's a strange and captivating idea, and a great way to understand it is by comparing it to the colorful chaos of Mario Kart. Just like you navigate the unpredictable mayhem of Rainbow Road, we need to find ways to navigate the unexpected turns of life.

Think about the power-ups. Remember when you grab that shiny star that makes you invincible? In our lives, we often encounter our own power-ups, those moments of encouragement or support from friends that give us the boost we need to tackle challenges. Maybe it's a motivating pep talk from a friend before an important presentation or a funny meme that reminds you to not take life too seriously. These uplifting moments come in many forms and help us face the chaos with renewed energy.

Now, let's dive into some strategies we can use to stay on track, inspired by our Mario Kart adventures. First, let's talk about learning to read the track. In Mario Kart, experienced players can predict the twists and turns of Rainbow Road. They know where the sharp corners are and when to slow down to avoid a crash. Similarly, in life, developing awareness is key. It means recognizing potential obstacles before they become overwhelming.

For example, imagine feeling buried under a long to-do list. Instead of viewing it as an impossible race, take a step back and assess what's really going on. Identify the most urgent tasks and see what can wait. By breaking it down into smaller, manageable parts, you create your own shortcuts, effectively steering through the chaos without veering off course.

Next, we have the skill of adaptability. Just like a Mario Kart player must constantly change their strategy based on the race's ups and downs—like dodging shells or adjusting after a sudden fall—we too need to learn to adjust in our lives. Suppose you've spent weeks preparing for a presentation, only to discover your audience has changed. Instead of panicking like you just hit a banana peel, take a deep breath and rethink your approach. Embrace the chaos, and adjust your message to fit the new situation.

This adaptability can also come from having a sense of humor. When life throws a curveball, laughter can be your best friend. Picture yourself racing down Rainbow Road, hitting a jump, only to land right in front of another racer who sends you flying off the track. It's frustrating, no doubt, but if you can laugh it off and realize that it's just part of the game, you'll be more likely to recover and keep racing.

Similarly, life often throws unexpected challenges our way that can feel annoying but can be viewed with a sense of humor. For instance, if you spill coffee on an important document just before a meeting, instead of letting panic take over, you could laugh about it, making light of the situation and reminding yourself that it's just another hurdle to get over.

Humor acts as a secret weapon, giving you the strength to bounce back.

Additionally, don't underestimate the power of friendship. Think back to those awesome multiplayer sessions in Mario Kart. Remember how exciting it felt to race alongside your friends, all of you navigating the tricky track together? When someone gets knocked off the edge, you all share a laugh, and when one person grabs a power-up, it feels like a win for the entire team.

In life, we can find that same supportive network in our friends, family, or coworkers. Don't hesitate to lean on those around you. Seek help when life feels overwhelming or when you sense you might tip over the edge. Just as you would cheer for your friends during a race, surround yourself with people who lift you up and help you stay in the game.

And let's not overlook the value of hitting the "reset" button. We all have moments when we become overwhelmed by the chaos and need to step back. In Mario Kart, hitting the reset button after a challenging round allows you to start fresh with a clearer mindset. Apply this idea to your life by recognizing when you need a breather. Whether it's taking a few moments away from a stressful task for a little reflection or treating yourself to a fun night out with friends, give yourself permission to reset.

Now, let's take a moment to consider what all of this means in the bigger picture. Life is often a chaotic race, much like Rainbow Road. It's filled with unexpected challenges, sharp turns, and the occasional banana peel. But through humor, adaptability, friendship, and self-compassion, we can navigate the chaos gracefully.

So, the next time you find yourself careening off the edge—whether in a game or in real life—remember that setbacks are just part of the journey. Embrace the chaos, laugh at the misadventures, and take a moment to reset. Each challenge becomes a chance for growth, and every obstacle teaches us something new.

Ultimately, the spirit of quantum tunneling reflects our experiences navigating the unpredictable paths of life. Just as particles can slip past barriers, we too can find our way through the chaos, adapting and laughing along the way. So grab that controller, my friend, and let's keep racing through this vibrant, wacky journey together. Life is a game, and with the right mindset, we can all reach the finish line—hopefully without falling off the edge!

The Idiot's Guide to Quantum Physics

Chapter 6: Multiverse Theory: The Infinite You

Imagine waking up one morning and deciding what socks to wear. You stand in front of your drawer, a doorway to alternate realities, facing the classic dilemma: blue or red? Let's take a moment to explore this seemingly small decision. According to the mind-blowing idea of multiverse theory, your choice right here, right now, isn't just about fashion—it's a cosmic crossroads that could create entire universes. Yes, you heard that right! As you slide into your blue socks, somewhere out there, in another lively dimension, another version of you is confidently wearing those red socks like a true rebel.

In that alternate universe, your fashion choices might be different, but you might also be a quirky trendsetter, turning mismatched socks into the next big thing. Picture this: you strike a pose for a viral Instagram post, and suddenly, the internet is buzzing with the hashtag #SockRevolution. Meanwhile, your blue-socked counterpart is busy arguing with socks-and-sandals enthusiasts in a heated online forum. This single choice—and the hilariously different realities it creates—

captures the essence of the many-worlds interpretation of quantum mechanics.

To dig deeper, let's break down the science behind this. The many-worlds interpretation, suggested by physicist Hugh Everett III in 1957, proposes that every time a quantum event happens—like a cat deciding whether to take a nap or knock over a vase—an entirely new universe comes to life. Each universe represents a different outcome, where that cat could end up as a world-famous vase-smashing champion, while in another universe, it chooses to become a zen meditation guru. It's a wild cosmic game of "what if" that turns our everyday decisions into a parade of infinite possibilities.

Now, let's think about the bigger picture of multiverse theory. Imagine it as a cosmic choose-your-own-adventure story, where every decision you make leads you down a new path. You might become a rock star in one universe, belting out songs that shake the music industry to its core. In another universe, you could be a potato farmer, growing the best spuds. And in yet another, you might even be a galactic ruler, overseeing a civilization of sentient jelly beans. The choices we make—or don't make—open the door to countless alternate selves, each with their own unique stories and quirks.

But it's not just scientists who find the idea of alternate realities fascinating. Pop culture has embraced the multiverse concept wholeheartedly, creating stories that tap into our curiosity about "what could have been." Ever watched a superhero movie? They're practically factories for multiverses! Take the Marvel Cinematic Universe, for instance, where Spider-Man swings between dimensions, meeting different versions of himself—from the perpetually tired Peter B. Parker to the super-cool Spider-Gwen. Each character showcases the different choices and circumstances we all face in life.

The multiverse idea also pops up in animated series, where characters encounter bizarre alternate versions of themselves. Consider "Rick and Morty." This show cranks up the multiverse concept to the max, with Rick, a brilliant scientist, hopping through countless dimensions, meeting everything from sentient pickles to anthropomorphic cats who have built their own civilization. Each episode humorously explores choice and consequence, where the stakes are absurd yet strangely relatable.

It's worth mentioning that while the multiverse theory is full of possibilities, it can also be overwhelming. If every choice we make creates a new universe, we're left with a dizzying array of options—enough to make even the most decisive person rethink their decisions. What if, in a parallel universe, you chose to study neuroscience instead of English literature? What if you never took that left turn and ended up thriving as a llama farmer in a picturesque mountain town? The sheer number of alternate realities can make our heads spin faster than a quantum particle caught in superposition.

Yet, as we ponder the chaos of infinite possibilities, we should remember that every choice—even the smallest ones—holds significance. They shape our lives and narratives. In this light, multiverse theory serves as a metaphor for life itself. We often find ourselves standing at crossroads, making decisions that ripple through our existence in ways we might never fully grasp. Just one tiny decision—a choice of socks, a casual dinner invitation—could set us on a totally different path, influencing who we become.

The beauty of multiverse theory lies not only in its scientific implications but also in its ability to spark our imagination. It invites us to ponder the oddities of life and embrace the unpredictability of our journeys. With this perspective, we can chuckle at the thought of our alternate selves, each one exploring the wacky outcomes of choices made and not made. Because honestly, who wouldn't find it funny to imagine a parallel life where you're the queen of potatoes, reigning over a kingdom of tubers, complete with a crown made of golden fries?

As we dive deeper into this whimsical theory, we discover a common thread: our lives are intertwined with choices that generate countless experiences. The multiverse isn't just a scientific notion; it's a playful reminder of the endless potential hidden within our everyday decisions. So next time you find yourself contemplating the color of your socks, take a moment to grin. Because in one universe, you might just be strutting your stuff in those mismatched beauties, becoming a trendsetter in a dimension where socks hold the keys to intergalactic diplomacy.

Superheroes and Quantum Realities

When we think about superheroes, we often picture caped champions flying through the air, fighting wicked villains with crazy powers. But as we flip through colorful comic pages and watch our favorite movies, we can't help but notice a fun twist: the multiverse. This fantastic idea doesn't just add spice to the stories of our cherished heroes; it also lets us take a playful look at our own lives, choices, and the crazy complexities of existence.

    Let's consider Spider-Man for a moment. This beloved web-slinger has jumped through more alternate realities than most of us can keep track of. There's Peter Parker, the classic nerd-turned-hero, swinging through the bustling streets of New York City. Then we have Miles Morales, a young kid who shows us that anyone can wear the mask. And we can't forget about Spider-Gwen, who comes from a world where she, not Peter, got bitten by that radioactive spider. Each version reflects different choices and experiences, not to mention a wild variety of costume designs! You've got to admire a hero who can rock both a red and blue suit and a trendy hoodie while still saving the day.

    The concept of the multiverse in superhero stories isn't just a clever trick; it also gives us a glimpse into the ideas behind chaos theory and quantum mechanics. Just imagine if every choice Peter Parker made created a new reality. In one universe, he might have outsmarted the Green Goblin using his brains instead of his webs, resulting in a life where he never held onto his powers out of responsibility and became a successful engineer instead. In another reality, he could have followed in Uncle Ben's footsteps and become a beloved social worker in New York, helping people all day long. These endless possibilities show how even the smallest decisions can create entire worlds.

Comic book writers and filmmakers have turned into modern philosophers, pondering the ideas of identity and self. The core of a hero's identity often hinges on their choices, and in the multiverse, each choice gives rise to a new version of that hero. It's not just Peter Parker experiencing this fun buffet of existence—Batman, Superman, and the X-Men all have their own multiversal stories, each dealing with the choices that shape who they are. It's like a cosmic game of "Choose Your Own Adventure," where heroes can live out a never-ending cycle of what-ifs, delighting fans who love to imagine alternate storylines.

Of course, this playful exploration of different realities can lead to some hearty laughs. Some superhero stories take the multiverse idea to wild extremes, creating plots that make you wonder if the writers were just tossing ideas around like confetti. "How about this: in one universe, Superman is a janitor? And in another, he's a world-famous chef?" You can almost hear the brainstorming session buzzing as they come up with increasingly outrageous scenarios. Yet, the silliness is part of the fun, as these colorful tales poke lighthearted fun at serious scientific theories while inviting us to explore our own imaginations.

A great example of this is the animated show "Rick and Morty," which masterfully weaves the multiverse into its wild stories. With Rick Sanchez, the quirky genius scientist, leading the pack, the show sends its characters flying through a whirlwind of dimensions filled with hilarious and often bizarre versions of themselves. In one episode, Morty meets an alternate version of his grandfather, who just happens to be a friendly potato that has achieved interstellar consciousness. It sounds completely ridiculous, yet this far-fetched idea provides a backdrop for exploring deeper themes of identity, choice, and consequence. Each strange scenario reflects the chaos of existence, and the humor lies in the wackiness of it all.

The multiverse isn't just a playground for the odd and funny; it also sparks some thought-provoking questions. If there are infinite versions of ourselves, what does that say about our choices and identities? In one universe, you might be a celebrated artist, while in another, you could be a down-on-his-luck eSports player constantly battling bad luck. Every alternate self acts like a mirror, reflecting the decisions we make and the paths we choose. For every success, there's a failure; for every happy moment, a heartbreak.

While superheroes represent exaggerated versions of multiverse stories, they also remind us of our potential and the importance of our choices. On days when we feel like we're just dragging through life in our pajamas, we can take comfort in knowing that somewhere in an alternate universe, we might be living our best lives, running marathons or leading world-changing projects. This thought helps us embrace our quirks and differences, realizing that every version of ourselves—whether a superhero, a potato farmer, or even an unhappy office worker—has its own unique worth.

As we journey through the wild and wacky worlds of superheroes, we can't help but laugh at the absurdity of it all. The multiverse encourages us not to take life too seriously, reminding us that in one reality, you might be saving the world while in another, you're just trying to remember where you left your keys. But the fun doesn't stop there. These stories spark our curiosity and inspire us to think about how science and creativity intersect. They give us the chance to consider the potential behind every choice we make.

In a nutshell, the superhero multiverse serves as a cultural mirror, reflecting our own complexities. It nudges us to think about the wild possibilities life can offer and to smile when we realize that our choices—big or small—are what truly define us. The next time you crack open a comic book or catch the latest superhero movie, take a moment to appreciate the intricate dance of alternate realities unfolding before your eyes. You might discover that the journey of your favorite hero resonates with your own, revealing the universal truths that connect us all—like a cosmic web spun by countless Spider-People, each playing their part in the grand design of destiny.

So, let's raise a metaphorical toast to the superheroes of the multiverse: those brave souls who leap through dimensions, reminding us to embrace our choices and the unpredictable nature of life. Whether they wear capes, tights, or even crowns made of golden fries, they are, at their core, reflections of us all—each one a symbol of the limitless possibilities of existence. And who wouldn't chuckle at the thought of being the ruler of a potato kingdom, where the biggest issue is ensuring the perfect fry-to-ratio at every feast? After all, in a universe filled with alternate realities, anything is possible, and laughter truly is the greatest superpower.

Your Alter-Ego Across Universes

Imagine waking up one day and looking in the mirror to see a version of yourself that made completely different choices. Instead of heading to that boring desk job, maybe this alternate you decided to train cats for a living, or perhaps they chose to dance ballet instead of playing soccer as a kid. The possibilities are limitless, and every little decision can lead to a brand-new reality.

In the grand scheme of the multiverse, each choice we make branches out into a different dimension. It's like life is a giant tree with branches that twist and turn, sprouting new leaves with each decision. Maybe one morning you brushed your teeth and skipped breakfast, leading to a typical Tuesday. In another universe, though, you lingered over a delicious breakfast burrito, turning your whole day into a tasty adventure filled with spicy salsa and unexpected fun. The wildness of this idea is both amusing and thought-provoking, like a cosmic version of the game "What If?" where the stakes are high, but the possibilities are delightfully silly.

Let's take a stroll through these imaginative alternate realities. Picture yourself as an intergalactic chef, whipping up alien dishes that no human has ever dared to try. You're grilling space nachos with glimmering stardust cheese and using a rare mineral from a comet as your secret ingredient. Imagine garnishing dishes for Martian diplomats while juggling the chaos of your kitchen. This life is all about crazy culinary adventures, mind-bending recipes, and keeping your cool when an extraterrestrial critic isn't impressed with your latest creation.

Or imagine being a dog-walker in a world where pets can talk back. You might find yourself saying, "Okay, Fido, I get that you want to chase that squirrel, but let's make a deal," as you squat down to chat with your furry client. Each dog would have its own personality, leading to a whirlwind of funny conversations as you try to negotiate their whims. "You can sniff that bush for five more minutes, but only if you promise not to pull on the leash." You could even become a low-key dog whisperer, building a community for four-legged friends and their humans while sharing your adventures online.

Now, let's shift gears and look at some more ordinary realities. In one universe, perhaps you never learned to ride a bike. Yes, you could be that adult still wobbling around, clinging to the handlebars like they're your lifeline. Picture yourself at the park, perched awkwardly on a bike that feels like a wild stallion trying to escape. Instead of speeding down the path with the wind in your hair, you're on training wheels, trying to regain your balance while your friends cheer you on. Each tumble and crash becomes a laugh fest, earning you the nickname "Bike Blunderer" among your friends. Who knew that a simple stumble could turn into such a source of joy and countless stories over pizza?

On the other hand, let's imagine a universe where you mastered bike riding and became a world-class stunt cyclist, wowing crowds with jaw-dropping tricks and gravity-defying jumps. You'd be the superhero of cycling, soaring through the air, performing crazy flips, and leaving audiences in awe. Think about the rush of adrenaline when you land a perfect backflip, with the crowd erupting in applause. It's fascinating to think how a simple misstep could've changed the entire course of your life.

Exploring these alternate realities isn't just about having a laugh; it also encourages us to reflect on who we are, our dreams, and the choices that shape our lives. Each version of ourselves carries different ambitions, fears, and quirks. Maybe you always dreamt of being an artist, but chose a stable corporate job instead. In another universe, you might have taken that leap, becoming a painter with work displayed in galleries all over the world. Can you imagine the joy of painting freely while sipping a glass of wine, surrounded by fellow creatives who inspire you? Your alternate self serves as a reminder that the paintbrush and canvas could have been your ticket to happiness.

Think about a version of you who fully embraced the digital age, becoming an influencer known for your unique take on life. You could have a series of viral dance videos, showcasing not just your questionable moves but also your quirky take on everyday challenges. "Watch me try to cook while doing the Macarena; it's bound to be a disaster!" Each post would be a slice of your life, filled with laughter, daily struggles, and the occasional burnt dinner. Your followers would appreciate your authenticity, loving every candid moment that highlights the hilarity of life.

Now let's dream up a more outrageous alternate self. Imagine a world where you became a professional cat trainer, teaching cats to perform incredible tricks. Your life turns into a cat circus, with feline acrobats jumping through hoops while you proudly guide them through stunning stunts. "And now, ladies and gentlemen, get ready for the phenomenal Mr. Whiskers as he conquers the world's tallest scratching post!" The audience gasps as Mr. Whiskers takes a daring leap. You laugh, knowing your days are filled with cat antics, treats, and moments of applause.

In this cat-centric universe, you also face the hilarious challenges of your job. Picture trying to teach a stubborn tabby to balance a ball on its nose while a playful Siamese insists on photobombing every training session. Social media becomes your playground for sharing cat-related fun, as you post videos of furry fails and triumphs. Your followers eagerly await each new adventure from your talented feline cast.

Exploring these alternate selves can lead to meaningful insights about our current lives. While we giggle at the craziness of these imagined careers, we might uncover dreams we've tucked away. Maybe the thought of being a cat trainer resonates with your love for animals, or the idea of stunt cycling reignites that long-forgotten passion for adventure. The multiverse invites us to reflect on our choices, encouraging us to think about how we can bring a little of our alternate selves into our everyday lives.

As we hop around the multiverse, it's hard not to laugh at the ridiculousness of it all. Life is a wild journey, filled with unexpected twists and funny scenarios that remind us not to take ourselves too seriously. We are all complex beings, shaped by our choices, dreams, and yes, sometimes our own silliness. Embracing the humor in our alternate realities helps us find joy in our quirks and imperfections, all while celebrating the beauty of life's unpredictability.

So here's to the countless versions of ourselves—the cat trainers, the stunt cyclists, the artists, and the influencers. Each alter-ego teaches us something valuable about who we are and the choices we make every single day. As we navigate through this delightful chaos called life, let's remember to enjoy the wild possibilities that come our way. After all, in the vast multiverse, you might just be living your best life somewhere else—possibly as a potato king, ruling over a kingdom of fries and ketchup!

Theodore Trudeau

Chapter 7: Quantum Mechanics for the Procrastinator

In the vast world of procrastination, we often find ourselves caught in a whirlwind of indecision that could easily match the wild movements of quantum particles. Imagine a particle zipping through the uncertainty of space, darting this way and that, existing in a state of possibility until we finally take a look and its chaotic wave function collapses into a single moment. Now, picture yourself standing in front of a never-ending to-do list that seems to grow longer and more overwhelming by the minute, jumping from one distracting choice to another while insecurity looms above like a heavy cloud. The similarities are striking, if not downright funny.

Let's take a moment to think about the classic struggle of a college student—truly the poster child for procrastination. Imagine it's just two days before finals, and you're sitting in your room, staring blankly at the walls as thoughts of study materials swirl around your mind. What should you do? It seems like the perfect time to tackle that mountain of laundry that's been piling up like a suburban version of Everest. What starts as a simple distraction quickly turns into an all-out cleaning spree. In this chaotic dance of procrastination, you find yourself in a state of superposition: you could be studying, but instead, you're knee-deep in laundry, dusting, or even rearranging your furniture. Every little decision—should I use fabric softener?—takes on the weight of a quantum event, clashing and collapsing into one reality.

Now we find ourselves facing choices that seem to multiply like crazy, much like the different spins and flips a quantum particle can take in its seemingly random path. A procrastinator's mind is like a particle accelerator, darting from one thought to another without a care for where it might end up. You could be cracking open your textbook, but instead, you get caught watching cat videos—an adorable diversion that does nothing for your GPA. And just like in the quantum world, this decision-making is filled with uncertainty. As you hover over the "Play" button, you might even start to wonder if these kittens are giving you important life lessons or just serving as a perfect excuse to procrastinate.

The unpredictability of quantum particles mirrors our own lives, as we bounce between tasks and often choose the least productive option simply because it feels more rewarding in the moment. Think about how quantum particles exist in a cloud of possibilities, unable to be pinned down until we take a closer look. As procrastinators, we find ourselves in a similar flux. You could be working diligently on that project, but instead, you're scrolling through Twitter, realizing that your focus is as unstable as a particle caught in a double-slit experiment. Each scroll introduces a new set of distractions, much like a particle slipping through various paths, only to be noticed at the last moment—a moment that might reveal your productivity has vanished, leaving you with nothing but memes and hashtags.

But what makes procrastination so tempting? Well, it's not just the joy of dodging responsibility. There's a certain thrill in the chaotic randomness of it all. Like quantum particles, there's a certain beauty in this disorder that many of us find strangely comforting. Our minds, like those particles, are constantly shifting, bouncing between tasks, wishes, and distractions. This back-and-forth can remind us of the quantum principle of uncertainty; we might not know exactly what we're doing, but that doesn't stop us from diving headfirst into the delightful chaos of our thoughts.

Let's not overlook the long list of tasks awaiting us, each with its own set of probabilities. You could tackle that report due tomorrow, but the pull of cleaning out your refrigerator, an activity both boring and unnecessary, is just too hard to resist. Your fridge becomes a black hole, drawing you in with the promise of forgotten leftovers and expired condiments. Meanwhile, the report sits quietly in the back of your mind, much like a particle waiting to be measured—definitely there, but just not in the spotlight.

In the world of quantum mechanics, particles can exist in multiple states at once, which is a concept called superposition. Think of it as a procrastinator's dream: you could be doing any number of productive things, yet you find yourself stuck in that hazy space of indecision. With each passing hour, the weight of your uncompleted tasks grows heavier, yet you remain anchored in this potentiality, caught between choices you're reluctant to make.

Whether you're binge-watching a new series or getting lost in the maze of online shopping, the procrastinator's world is where every decision feels significant, yet every action seems to pull you further away from productivity. Just like quantum particles, we navigate an intricate maze of choices, fully aware that each one could lead to either a productive outcome or a delightful distraction. In this drama of procrastination, we are both the watcher and the watched, shifting into one state or another based on whatever whim captures our attention.

The randomness seen in quantum mechanics can be seen in our own decision-making too. Just like the unpredictable paths of particles, our choices often lead us down winding roads of procrastination we never meant to travel. Ask any procrastinator about the wildest activities they've done while avoiding work, and you'll hear a treasure trove of stories. For example, you might find someone knee-deep in a DIY project for a Pinterest-inspired bookshelf when all they wanted to do was write a paper. What started as a good idea can quickly spiral into a rabbit hole of randomness, where paintbrushes and wood glue take precedence over the written word.

As we navigate the often chaotic waters of procrastination, it's helpful to recognize the humor in our erratic behavior. While we may not be quantum particles zipping through the universe, our thought processes can be just as unpredictable. Next time you find yourself stuck in a procrastination spiral, remind yourself that even the most chaotic particle has a place in the universe. There's a delicate balance between chaos and order, just like in quantum mechanics. And perhaps, seeing the silliness in our choices can bring a smile to our faces and help us embrace the delightful unpredictability of life.

So, the next time you feel overwhelmed by your to-do list, remember that even the simplest tasks can lead to a cascade of distractions and quirky decisions. Welcome to the procrastinator's universe, where you are both a player and an audience, caught in the wild whirlwind of choices. Embrace your inner particle, enjoy the randomness, and maybe—just maybe—find a moment of productivity before getting swept away in another binge-watching session. After all, like in quantum mechanics, the chance to do the right thing is always there, just waiting for you to notice it.

Double-Slit Experiment with Social Media Drama

Picture this: a physics experiment that has puzzled scientists and sparked endless discussions about the nature of reality itself. The double-slit experiment is where things get really strange and wonderfully intriguing. In this experiment, a beam of particles, like electrons or photons, is shot at a barrier with two narrow slits. Now, if we watch the particles as they pass through the slits, they behave like individual particles, leaving behind two distinct patterns on a screen behind the barrier. Seems straightforward, right? But here's the twist: when no one is watching—when no measurements are made—the particles mysteriously act like waves and create an interference pattern that suggests they've passed through both slits at the same time. It's like they're throwing a wild party when we're not looking!

This amazing discovery brings up some deep questions about the nature of observation and reality itself. How can particles exist in a state of possibility, acting both as waves and particles depending solely on whether someone is observing? It's almost as if the particles are saying, "We'll keep it mysterious until you pay attention!" Essentially, the simple act of watching seems to push these particles into a definite state, turning their potential into something real and measurable. It's a graceful dance of uncertainty, one that reflects the complexities of human interactions in our online lives.

Now, let's shift gears from the world of quantum physics to the realm of social media. Just like the particles in the double-slit experiment, our online identities can change based on who's observing us. Ever notice how your Twitter voice can be a bit sassier than your Instagram self, while your LinkedIn profile is all about being professional? We carefully shape these different versions of ourselves, creating an online presence that matches the expectations of each platform. It's like putting on a performance, where sharing our lives becomes a tricky balancing act similar to how particles navigate their dual nature.

Imagine walking into a party without knowing who else is there. As you step in, you can feel the pressure to act a certain way. Are you the funny one, the smart one, or the ambitious go-getter? Depending on who's in the room, your persona might shift instantly, adapting to the vibe like those particles sliding through the slits. It's an amusing analogy—like quantum particles, we also wobble between different versions of ourselves based on our audience.

The Idiot's Guide to Quantum Physics

As we navigate the bustling world of social media, we master the art of presenting ourselves in ways that would impress even the most seasoned physicist. We might post that perfectly staged selfie on Instagram, complete with a motivational quote, while simultaneously getting into a witty debate on Twitter. Our online actions become a colorful mix of identities, each one carefully crafted to grab attention and spark reactions. It's like a digital masquerade, where everyone wears their chosen masks, ready to dance to the beats of likes, retweets, and comments.

The humor in this social media drama isn't lost on us. We've all seen those cringe-worthy moments when someone's carefully constructed online persona falls apart under the weight of reality. Think of the classic case of a "wellness influencer" posting a picture of their beautifully arranged avocado toast while secretly munching on a bag of chips later. It's the timeless struggle of maintaining that perfect image while real life unfolds like a sitcom with poorly timed jokes. Just like quantum particles caught between states, our online lives constantly juggle between being real and being a performance.

But the unpredictable nature of social media doesn't stop there. Just as the double-slit experiment shows that observation changes outcomes, the reactions of our followers also influence our online behavior. A simple like or share can lead us on a path of self-doubt or validation. We often find ourselves adjusting our online personas based on how much engagement we get, much like a particle nervously shifting as its wave function collapses. It's ironic! In this digital age, we might be more aware of our audience than ever, yet the chance of being misunderstood is just as high.

Take memes, for instance. A well-timed meme can capture a complex idea in a single image, often making us laugh or nod in agreement. But what happens when our attempts at humor flop? Suddenly, our clever caption meant to go viral becomes a confusing riddle for the reader. Confusion reigns, much like the initial surprise we feel when grappling with the wave-particle duality. It's a funny reminder of how our best efforts can sometimes miss the mark in a world where the rules of engagement keep changing.

And let's not overlook the unexpected consequences of our online performances.

Similar to how the double-slit experiment can lead to misunderstandings about how particles behave, our carefully curated online selves can create a haze of confusion for those around us. We've all had moments when someone brings up a post or comment from weeks ago, and we're left scratching our heads, wondering which version of ourselves they're talking about. It's a silly game of "Who said what when?" that could rival the complexities of quantum entanglement.

Amid this dance of online identities, we sometimes overlook the beauty of being authentic. In a world where everyone strives to showcase their best selves, there's something refreshing about just being who we are, flaws and all. Just as particles remind us of the duality of existence, our online lives can serve as a powerful reminder that we're all just trying to find our way through the messy landscape of identity. So why not share those less-than-perfect moments? They could resonate with someone scrolling through their feed, creating a connection that goes beyond the polished perfection.

As we consider the double-slit experiment and its meaning, let's appreciate the humor and unpredictability that come with our online interactions. The relationship between observer and observed carries the same weight in our social lives as it does in the quantum world. We are all part of this grand experiment, navigating the ebb and flow of our identities while embracing the absurdity of it all.

So the next time you're curating an Instagram story or crafting a Twitter thread, take a moment to reflect on the cosmic joke playing out around you. Just like those particles caught in a never-ending dance of possibilities, you too are exploring a universe of identities shaped by the people watching. Embrace the chaos, enjoy the unpredictability, and remember that, at the end of the day, we're all just trying to make sense of our place in this wild, wonderful world—one meme, one post, and one laugh at a time.

Quantum Nonchalance in Life

Life is a wild ride, full of surprises that can feel like a chaotic science experiment. Picture a family dinner: a gathering of loved ones, filled with laughter and delicious food. But if you look closely, there's a tangled mess of expectations, differing opinions, and the constant chance that a single comment could spark a lively debate. Just like particles in a quantum state, each family member has their own unique quirks, creating an atmosphere buzzing with both tension and humor.

Take Aunt Linda, for example. She's the self-proclaimed family chef who presents her latest dish with all the confidence of a particle entering a tricky experiment—steady until someone takes notice. "I've outdone myself this time! This quiche is the best you'll ever taste!" she exclaims, beaming beside her culinary creation. But the moment Cousin Billy takes a bite and raises an eyebrow, the mood shifts. Suddenly, Aunt Linda's confidence wavers, as if her quiche has flipped from a glorious triumph to a potential disaster. "Is it too salty?" she asks, her voice quaking with doubt. Now, the dinner table mirrors the unpredictable world of quantum mechanics—a swirl of reactions and outcomes.

This is where the quantum analogy really shines. Just like particles that are always in flux, our interactions during family gatherings are constantly shifting. Aunt Linda's moment of pride could quickly spiral into a debate about her cooking skills, reflecting how particles change based on who's observing them. If no one had dared to taste her dish, Aunt Linda might have blissfully remained unaware of the storm brewing over her quiche—or the storm brewing in her heart.

    Now, let's switch gears and think about a road trip as another character in this quirky drama of life. Road trips are meant to be filled with joy, laughter, and beautiful scenery, but they can also turn into chaotic decision-making adventures, much like the puzzles of quantum mechanics. Picture this: you're driving down a winding road when someone in the backseat suddenly shouts, "I need a snack!" At that moment, the universe splits into countless options. Do you stick to your planned route with that delicious lunch spot you found, or do you make a detour to the nearby gas station for a questionable assortment of snacks that may or may not be edible?

    In quantum mechanics, this moment reflects the concept of possibility. Just like particles that can be in multiple states until someone looks, your road trip is hanging in a balance of choices. The decision you make shifts the direction of the journey and changes how everyone in the car experiences it. Choosing the wholesome lunch spot might mean missing out on a spontaneous dance party fueled by gas station snacks, but it also spares you the regret of discovering mystery meat hiding in the backseat snack bag later on.

As life unfolds its unpredictable nature, we can learn to embrace this concept of quantum nonchalance. We often freeze up, worried about making the wrong choice, but it's that very uncertainty that makes life exciting. The unpredictable nature of our decisions, whether during family dinners or road trips, mirrors how quantum particles behave. By welcoming the chaos, we can create some of the most memorable experiences of our lives—even if they come with a sprinkle of unexpected drama.

Consider the classic family game night. The board is set, snacks are in place, and everyone is ready for some friendly competition. Yet, as the game progresses, tensions can rise, alliances may form and break, and the unpredictable nature of human interactions takes center stage. One minute, you're sharing a laugh with your sibling over a silly mistake, and the next, you're embroiled in a heated argument over the rules—just like particles in a quantum system influenced by who's watching.

In the spirit of quantum nonchalance, let's celebrate the beautiful messiness found in these chaotic moments. The best stories come from unexpected twists and turns that life throws our way. Maybe during that game night, you discover that your usually calm grandmother has a surprising competitive streak, leaving everyone in stitches. Or perhaps Cousin Sarah, who usually avoids conflict, becomes a fierce competitor, turning the game into a lively display of quick wit and playful banter.

The unpredictability of these interactions is much like how quantum particles behave—seemingly random yet perfectly organized within their own chaotic space. Just as scientists embrace the uncertainties of quantum mechanics, we too can find joy in life's unpredictability.

Having a good sense of humor is a crucial tool for navigating this wild terrain. Think about how memes have become a fun way to express our chaotic lives through a single image. A well-timed meme can capture the shared experience of uncertainty, turning complex feelings into something easy to digest. Memes act as a bridge, connecting our personal stories to a larger cultural narrative that embraces life's absurdities.

Imagine scrolling through your social media and stumbling upon a meme that perfectly captures the chaos of a family gathering gone wrong. Maybe it's a cartoon showing a dinner where the food is on fire, and everyone is arguing over the remote control. You laugh, recognizing the truth in the chaos, and share it with a caption that says, "Family dinners are like quantum physics: you never know what state they'll be in!"

In an instant, that simple meme captures the unpredictable nature of family interactions. In a world that often feels overwhelming, humor becomes our secret weapon, helping us cope with life's uncertainties in a way that is relatable and fun. These lighthearted moments invite us to embrace the unknown, encouraging us to take risks, learn from our mistakes, and share a laugh along the way.

The unpredictability of life isn't limited to family dinners and road trips; it weaves through every part of our experience. Think about the times you've taken a leap of faith—whether it's starting a new job, jumping into a relationship, or trying out a new hobby. Each decision carries a quantum potential, a myriad of outcomes ready to unfold. The true magic lies in embracing this uncertainty, just as scientists marvel at the mysteries of quantum mechanics.

Let's celebrate those moments when life throws us a curveball. Perhaps you decided on a whim to take a spontaneous trip to a new city without making any reservations. The thrill of the unknown leads you to discover a hidden gem, like an eccentric café tucked away in an alley that serves the most incredible pastries you've ever tasted. Your choice to dive into the unknown becomes a delightful adventure, reminding you that sometimes the best moments arise from a willingness to embrace unpredictability.

This idea of quantum nonchalance encourages us to shift how we think. Instead of seeing life's unpredictability as something to fear, we can view it as a chance for growth and discovery. Much like the quantum particles that flit between states, we can navigate the complexities of our lives with a sense of wonder and curiosity.

As we travel through the winding roads of life, it's all about how we respond to uncertainty. It's about turning chaos into a dance, allowing ourselves to sway with the rhythms of life instead of resisting them. Each twist and turn offers a chance to learn, adapt, and appreciate the beauty of the unknown.

So, next time you find yourself in a situation bursting with unpredictability—be it a family dinner, a road trip, or an impromptu adventure—remember to lean into the chaos. Embrace the quantum nonchalance life has to offer, and let laughter lead you through the unexpected. Life, with all its quirks and surprises, is an amazing journey we're all a part of.

With every choice we make, we join in on the cosmic joke that is existence, exploring a world that reflects the unpredictable yet beautiful nature of quantum mechanics. As we laugh, learn, and grow, let's cherish the unpredictability of our lives. It's within this chaos that we truly find the essence of being alive.

Theodore Trudeau

Chapter 8: Quantum Physics in Media: A Cultural Lens

In the vast world of animated TV, few shows have captured people's imaginations quite like *Rick and Morty*. With its offbeat humor, twisty stories, and wildly creative takes on science, it has turned into a beloved classic. But beyond the laughs and outrageous plots, the show offers a fascinating glimpse into the world of quantum physics. By mixing complicated ideas with outrageous comedy, *Rick and Morty* not only entertains but also teaches viewers about the strange and captivating concepts of quantum mechanics.

At the center of much of the series is the idea of the multiverse. This concept suggests that there are countless parallel realities where every possible outcome of every decision happens at the same time. It's a mind-blowing thought! Just imagine: every time you make a choice, no matter how small—like whether to grab a snack or binge-watch your favorite show—a new universe comes into being. In one of them, you might have gone to that party instead of staying home. This delightful absurdity is what *Rick and Morty* thrives on, and it presents the science behind it in a way that feels almost approachable.

One episode that beautifully illustrates this is "Rickmancing the Stone." In this adventure, Rick and Morty find themselves in a post-apocalyptic world that feels like something straight out of classic adventure films. Despite the chaotic setting, they meet a version of Morty's mom who has turned into a tough warrior. While this may seem far from a physics lab, the story reflects quantum ideas. The characters jump through different realities and make choices that lead to wildly different results, mirroring the idea of quantum superposition. In quantum physics, particles can be in multiple states at the same time until someone observes them, resulting in one specific outcome. In the *Rick and Morty* universe, each choice branches off into a new reality, creating a sprawling story filled with endless possibilities.

And who could forget Schrödinger's Cat? This thought experiment often pops up in talks about quantum mechanics. Simply put, it suggests that a cat inside a sealed box can be considered both alive and dead until someone opens the box to check. This idea raises profound questions about the nature of reality itself. *Rick and Morty* cleverly weaves this concept into their storytelling. One memorable moment shows a character who is both alive and dead until another character decides to check in on them, adding a comedic twist to an already complicated idea. This shows how the show transforms tough scientific concepts into fun and engaging stories that anyone can enjoy.

The characters in *Rick and Morty* often represent exaggerated scientific types. Rick Sanchez, the hard-drinking genius, is the ultimate mad scientist who captures the wild spirit of quantum theory. His unpredictable actions and reckless antics bring humor to serious ideas. Morty, his anxious and often clueless grandson, serves as a relatable sidekick, trying to make sense of the bizarre situations created by Rick's experiments. The dynamic between these two not only sets up hilarious moments but also helps introduce scientific concepts. When Rick explains quantum theory in a way that leaves Morty scratching his head, viewers get a funny yet insightful look at topics that might seem intimidating.

Throughout the series, the audience is treated to witty one-liners and clever jokes that sprinkle in scientific terms. One standout moment has Rick exclaiming, "Wubba Lubba

Dub Dub! I'm in great pain! Please help me!" While it's a funny line, it also hints at the existential worries that often come with exploring quantum mechanics. The blend of humor and deep thought is a hallmark of the show, encouraging viewers to engage with the content on different levels. At its heart, *Rick and Morty* shows that diving into scientific ideas doesn't have to be boring; it can be filled with laughter and silliness, too.

The influence of *Rick and Morty* on how people view quantum physics is huge. In today's world, where communicating science is more important than ever, the show has sparked discussions about topics that might otherwise stay in academic circles. Social media is buzzing with memes and conversations about the show, often highlighting its quirky take on scientific ideas. Fans share their favorite moments, chat about the implications of the multiverse, and wonder about the nature of reality—all while laughing at the wildness of it all. This cultural phenomenon has made quantum physics a popular topic, bridging the gap between complex science and everyday life.

As the show keeps evolving, its impact on pop culture and science education is likely to grow. The mix of humor and curiosity opens the door for audiences to explore the mysteries of the universe without feeling overwhelmed by the science. By simplifying quantum physics through the fun lens of a cartoon, *Rick and Morty* paves the way for a new generation of thinkers and dreamers who might just feel inspired to dive deeper into the world of science and exploration.

In a universe that often feels overwhelmingly complex, *Rick and Morty* reminds us that sometimes, the best way to grasp the complicated world of quantum mechanics is to embrace the absurd and have a good laugh along the way. Whether it's pondering the implications of parallel universes or just enjoying the wild adventures of a mad scientist and his unwilling sidekick, the show encourages viewers to step back and appreciate the crazy journey that is both quantum theory and the human experience. After all, if we can find humor in the mysterious, perhaps we can also discover connections to our own lives in the strange and wonderful dance of atoms and particles that shape our reality.

Marvel's Quantum Elements

As the Marvel Cinematic Universe (MCU) grows and changes, it invites audiences into the exciting and puzzling world of quantum physics. Watching the MCU isn't just about thrilling superhero action; it's also a chance to explore some of the most astonishing ideas in modern science. Take the Quantum Realm, for instance. It's a fascinating entry point into discussions about entanglement, non-locality, and the very nature of time and space. In this quirky realm, the rules of physics that we're used to are flipped upside down and shown through a captivating cinematic lens that blends entertainment with scientific wonder.

The Quantum Realm first popped up in the movie *Ant-Man*. Here, it serves not only as a key plot element but also as a stunning visual experience that has sparked excitement and conversation among fans and scientists alike. The filmmakers took creative risks with its vibrant, psychedelic visuals, presenting the Quantum Realm as a dazzling swirl of colors and shapes that challenge the norms of our everyday world. This imaginative take grabs our attention while giving a nod to the strange realities of quantum mechanics. The idea of shrinking down to such a tiny scale, leaving behind the physics we know, is thrilling for both casual viewers and science enthusiasts.

The Idiot's Guide to Quantum Physics

At its heart, the Quantum Realm embodies the principles of quantum entanglement and non-locality. To put it simply, entanglement is when particles connect in such a way that the state of one can instantly affect the other, no matter how far apart they are. It's a mind-bending concept. Imagine trying to explain to someone that two particles could be so closely linked that changing one will directly influence the other, even if they're light-years away! This idea resonates with the intricate relationships between heroes in the MCU, where actions in one setting can ripple through others.

In *Ant-Man*, the Quantum Realm takes on a comedic tone. Our hero, Scott Lang, shrinks down to a subatomic size, leading to a visual adventure that feels like a ride through a cosmic amusement park. The scenes burst with whimsical imagery that, while inspired by scientific concepts, focus on entertainment. This playful absurdity makes the complex ideas of quantum physics more accessible. By wrapping these concepts in a fantasy story, the filmmakers invite viewers to think about the possibilities of time travel and alternative realities without getting lost in the technical jargon that can often feel overwhelming.

The ideas of the Quantum Realm go beyond just what we see on screen. The topic of time travel, especially in *Avengers: Endgame*, adds a deeper layer to the discussion of quantum physics. The characters use the Quantum Realm to manipulate time, setting out on a quest to gather Infinity Stones from different points in history. Here, the MCU dives into the concept of time dilation—which is a fascinating part of quantum theory suggesting that time isn't fixed. It can stretch or shrink based on speed and gravity. The film cleverly weaves this idea into the familiar superhero storyline, showing how fantastical elements can help convey complex scientific themes.

As the story unfolds, manipulating time becomes a source of both humor and drama. The Avengers, using their knowledge of the Quantum Realm, confront their past selves and navigate the emotional fallout from changing timelines. The film balances the seriousness of these choices with humor—after all, what's funnier than watching characters deal with their own blunders in a comically ironic way? This blend of light-heartedness and deeper reflection is where Marvel shines, offering viewers a chance to think about serious themes while also enjoying the ride.

Furthermore, the superhero powers often mirror quantum phenomena, adding another interesting twist. Take Ant-Man's ability to shrink to the size of a particle. This power reflects the scaling ideas in quantum mechanics, where particles behave in strange and unexpected ways. The visual exaggeration of size, where something incredibly small can have a huge impact, serves as a metaphor for the often-overlooked details of quantum physics. It encourages the audience to think about how small changes can lead to big consequences—a theme common in both superhero tales and scientific inquiries.

The mix of humor and serious science is a key feature of the MCU. In a world where the stakes can be incredibly high, the films skillfully include moments of fun, ensuring that audiences aren't overwhelmed by heavy themes. This balance creates a unique viewing experience where laughter and deep thoughts about reality and the universe coexist. The playful nature of the characters, their witty exchanges, and the sheer absurdity of their situations remind us that even with complex discussions, there's always room for joy.

Memorable scenes from the films highlight this mix of serious and silly. One standout moment occurs during the planning of the time heist in *Endgame*. The characters engage in a humorous back-and-forth about the mechanics of time travel, filling their chatter with jokes and quips that lighten what could've been a heavy scientific explanation. Their interactions reflect real-life conversations, where humor helps break the tension and makes tough topics easier to understand. It's a clever tactic that keeps the audience engaged while subtly teaching them about the implications of quantum theories.

The impact of these films on popular culture is huge. As fans interact with the MCU, they often take to social media to share their excitement, confusion, and questions about the quantum elements presented in the films. Memes abound, offering funny takes on complex ideas, and conversations spark among fans dissecting the details of their favorite characters' journeys. This relatable humor surrounding grand themes encourages more people to join the discussion, bringing quantum physics into everyday chatter.

In addition, the films have sparked a wave of interest among younger viewers, inspiring them to explore scientific concepts that might have previously felt out of reach. Comic book fans can find themselves drawn to physics, and those who never considered studying science might become curious about the quantum mysteries beneath their favorite superhero stories. In this way, the MCU becomes more than just entertainment; it's a bridge connecting complex scientific ideas to popular culture.

As the MCU keeps evolving, so will its exploration of quantum themes. Future films are likely to dive even deeper into the implications of the Quantum Realm, exploring the unknown areas of science while keeping the humorous spirit that fans love. This blend of science fiction and comedy creates a space where audiences can tackle profound ideas without feeling overwhelmed.

The journey through Marvel's Quantum Elements is an exciting one, filled with thrills, laughter, and wonder. It invites viewers to think about the universe's mysteries while enjoying the antics of their favorite heroes. By weaving quantum themes into their stories, the MCU opens the door for rich discussions about science, reality, and the connections that tie us all together. So as we step away from the Quantum Realm, let's appreciate that in the Marvel universe, the complexities of quantum physics are not just academic—they're fantastic adventures waiting to be explored. What lies ahead in this ever-expanding universe of superhero stories is an exhilarating mystery, and we're on the edge, ready to discover the endless possibilities that quantum mechanics has to offer.

Media's Love for Quantum Quirks

In a world where science can feel like a far-off castle sitting on top of a mountain, only reachable by the most daring thinkers, quantum physics stands out as a particularly intriguing peak. People are naturally curious about this complicated area of study, and the media knows how to tap into that curiosity. From movies to TV shows, books, and even art, the quirky world of quantum mechanics is transformed into something that's not only easy to digest but also a lot of fun. The media's fascination with quantum physics seems to come from a deep desire to tackle some of life's biggest questions: uncertainty, reality, and the oddness of existence. These topics hit home for many, allowing for a rich exploration of what it means to live in a world that can be both puzzling and beautiful.

As humans, we have a strong attraction to the unknown, the mysterious, and the strange. Quantum mechanics captures this fascination perfectly. At the heart of quantum theory is the unsettling yet fascinating idea that particles can exist in multiple states at once until observed, much like Schrödinger's famous cat, which lives as both alive and dead until someone opens the box. This delightful paradox sparks our imagination and nudges us into deep thinking. And who better to unpack these exciting ideas than the media, which has a talent for breaking down complicated concepts into something we can all enjoy with a bowl of popcorn?

Movies like *Inception* and *Interstellar* take viewers on thrilling journeys through unreal dimensions and mind-bending timelines. These films invite us to join an adventure where fantasy meets science. In *Inception*, the layers of dreams within dreams echo the idea of multiple realities, each one following its own set of rules, just like the quantum world. The film encourages us to rethink our own understanding of reality, inviting us to engage playfully yet profoundly with the subject. It's as if filmmakers have opened a window into the quantum universe, letting us glimpse the madness that resides within.

Television series also jump into the mix, showcasing the quirky and sometimes whimsical sides of quantum physics. For instance, *Rick and Morty* blends humor and science fiction in a way that keeps us laughing while also making us think about life's bigger questions. The show's main characters—a mad scientist and his naive grandson—travel through different dimensions and timelines, encountering strange creatures and alternate realities that reflect quantum principles. The humor acts as a bridge, making the more unsettling parts of quantum theory easier to digest. Through its absurdity, the show invites viewers to embrace the weirdness while also encouraging them to reflect on the deeper questions of existence—a truly enjoyable combo.

Beyond films and TV, literature has also made its mark in the realm of quantum discussions. Books like *The Quantum Thief* by Hannu Rajaniemi and *Quantum Physics for Beginners* by Carl J. Johnson tackle the challenge of translating complex theories into gripping stories. They not only present the basics of quantum mechanics but also delve into the philosophical questions that arise: What is real? How do our perceptions shape our understanding of the universe? These authors skillfully blend scientific concepts with intriguing plots, allowing readers to engage with quantum ideas in a way that feels both entertaining and enlightening.

Art, too, plays a big role in the media's fascination with the quirks of quantum physics. Visual artists have long found inspiration in the abstract and often counterintuitive nature of this field. They explore light and shadow, dimensions, and uncertainty in their work, all while tackling the oddities of existence. These artists challenge us to see reality through a lens that embraces both chaos and beauty, reflecting the very principles that govern the quantum world. Art exhibits focused on quantum themes create a space for conversation and curiosity among audiences who might not typically dip their toes into the deeper waters of science.

As the internet continues to shape how we communicate, social media has become an important player in spreading the word about quantum physics. Memes, in particular, have cleverly used humor to bring complex scientific ideas into everyday discussions. There's a whole universe of viral memes about quantum mechanics, where clever captions meet images of Schrödinger's cat or famous physicist Richard Feynman. These funny snippets help to demystify the concepts while creating a shared language that connects science lovers with curious minds. Social media transforms once-confusing ideas into relatable, entertaining content, making it easier for everyone to dive deeper into the subject.

The rise of meme culture also highlights how the public interprets and sometimes misunderstands quantum theory. Memes often showcase the absurdities and paradoxes of quantum physics in a lighthearted way, inviting laughter and reflection. A meme featuring a bewildered cat captioned with "When you realize particles can exist in multiple states... what is reality?" resonates with anyone wrestling with life's perplexities. This playful take doesn't just entertain; it encourages more in-depth conversations about scientific theories, challenging all of us to rethink our understanding of the universe.

Moreover, these memes create a sense of community among those exploring the challenging terrain of quantum ideas. Quantum memes unite science enthusiasts, philosophers, and the curious alike, building a connection where humor becomes a bridge linking diverse perspectives. The shared laughter and engagement enrich discussions around science, making quantum physics feel more approachable and prompting questions that might otherwise seem daunting.

Ultimately, the media's fascination with quantum quirks serves an even bigger purpose: to simplify the complex world of quantum physics and make it relatable for everyone. The blend of humor and serious science eases the anxiety that often comes with tackling tough scientific concepts. When we can laugh at the absurdity of the universe, we open ourselves up to a world of curiosity and discovery. In a culture that increasingly values humor and connection, popular media plays a vital role in shaping how we understand the complexities around us.

By embracing the quirks of quantum physics in various forms of media, we cultivate a sense of wonder that goes beyond traditional academia, inviting everyone to explore the mysteries of existence. The mix of humor, relatability, and scientific inquiry creates a culture where the complexities of quantum mechanics are not just academic puzzles but exciting adventures waiting to be uncovered. So let's celebrate the media's love for quantum quirks, recognizing that within the world of entertainment, we can discover paths to wisdom, inquiry, and perhaps a deeper understanding of the universe we inhabit. As we navigate the fascinating realm of quantum mechanics, let's do so with a sense of humor, ready to embrace the delightful absurdities at the heart of science.

Chapter 9: Quantum Field Theory: Vibes and Energies

Imagine for a moment that the universe isn't just a collection of tiny, stubborn particles huddled together like commuters on a packed subway during rush hour. Instead, see it as a vast, lively quantum field—like the biggest dance floor you can think of, where energy flows and bounces through space and time, creating a beautiful rhythm that shapes reality itself. On this dance floor, each particle isn't just sitting still; it's more like a fleeting dance move that echoes the universe's underlying beat.

When we step onto this vibrant dance floor, it's crucial to recognize that the music playing—the quantum field—sets the vibe for everything that happens. The bass thumps with energy, streaming like a river of possibility. This rhythm creates a backdrop where particles come to life and interact with one another. Just like every dancer on the floor responds to the music, every particle in the universe reacts to the quantum field, adding to the fundamental interactions that create the world around us.

To make this more relatable, picture a lively party full of energy. Imagine you're surrounded by friends, the music booming from the speakers, and everyone's moving to the beat in their unique styles. Some are breakdancing, others are trying the cha-cha, and a few are swaying to their own groove. Each dancer symbolizes a particle, and their movements are influenced by the rhythm of the music—a perfect way to think about how particles interact with the quantum field.

In this cosmic celebration, every interaction counts. Think about a dance floor where one person's wild arm movements might accidentally bump into someone else, causing a ripple effect of laughter and a little chaos. In the same way, particles engage with one another in the quantum field, creating a symphony of reactions that can lead to surprises. One moment, you're boogieing to a funky beat, and the next, you find yourself in a hilarious dance-off. Similarly, in quantum field theory, particles can suddenly pop in and out of existence, making this cosmic dance unpredictable and full of delightful surprises.

Now you might be asking how this all ties back to our everyday world and, more importantly, to the very core of our reality. Let's take a moment to think about what this analogy means. The universe isn't just sitting still; it's always changing, much like the vibe of a party shifts over time. Remember how, at some parties, the energy dips during a slow song, only to explode back up when the DJ plays a classic dance hit? The quantum field works similarly, where fluctuations create a network of connections—one particle's movement affects another, which influences yet another, and so on.

But the quirky nature of this quantum dance doesn't stop with simple interactions. The quantum field also gives rise to the strange phenomenon of existence itself. Think of a cute cat video that suddenly goes viral. One moment, it's just a playful clip of a kitten with a ball of yarn, and in the blink of an eye, it's all over social media, racking up millions of views and spawning dozens of memes. What's the link here? Just like the unexpected fame of that cat video captures everyone's attention, quantum fields operate in a similarly surprising way. The very fabric of our reality can create particles and energy from the field, showing up in ways as unexpected as a cat tumbling off a windowsill in slow motion.

Yet, even with all this fun imagery, we shouldn't overlook the scientific clarity in the mix. Quantum field theory teaches us that particles aren't just solid objects taking up space. They are actually excitations of the fields that fill the universe. This gives rise to two important ideas: particles and fields are linked in a dance that defines everything around us. The dance floor itself—the quantum field—always exists, while the dancers (particles) join in when energy fluctuations invite them to the party.

This connection offers a neat explanation for the forces that govern the universe, including gravity and electromagnetism. Picture gravity as an overly enthusiastic partygoer, pulling everyone closer together, while electromagnetic forces create a fun game of attraction and repulsion, drawing some dancers together while pushing others apart. This dynamic interplay forms the universe we know, where energy flows like a river, and the dance never truly stops.

As we navigate this lively dance floor of existence, we start to see that everything is connected—each movement, each interaction shapes not just the individual but the entire group. The cosmic dance of the quantum field reflects a deeper truth about our universe: it isn't a collection of isolated pieces but a vast web of interconnected energy vibes that shape relationships, behaviors, and the reality we experience.

Grasping this dance invites us to rethink our place in the cosmos. Just as each dancer adds to the overall mood of the party, every particle plays its part in the grand choreography of the universe. The relentless energy of the quantum field flows through everything, reminding us that we aren't separate from this dance; we're a vital part of it.

So, the next time you find yourself mulling over the universe's mysteries, remember that we're all dancers on this grand cosmic stage, moving to the rhythm of a music that is as unpredictable as it is beautiful. Embracing the joy of this idea can help us appreciate the deep complexities of quantum mechanics, allowing us to navigate the unpredictable beats of life with laughter, curiosity, and a sense of connection to everything around us.

In this dynamic dance of particles and fields, we have the chance to explore the very essence of our reality. The quantum field isn't just a distant concept buried in textbooks; it's a lively, breathing aspect of our universe. Just like every great party comes with its surprises, the quantum realm is filled with delightful mysteries waiting for us to uncover, inviting us all to join in the dance of existence.

So let's step onto the dance floor together, feel the vibes of the quantum field, and let ourselves be swept away in the cosmic rhythm of the universe. After all, life is too short to stand on the sidelines when the music is playing and the possibilities are boundless.

Particles vs. Fields

Have you ever been to a Broadway show and found yourself not just mesmerized by the lead actors, but also by the incredible team of stagehands, lighting technicians, and set designers who work tirelessly behind the scenes? While the spotlight shines on the main performers, it's those behind-the-scenes heroes who make sure everything runs smoothly and every moment feels just right. Similarly, in the world of quantum physics, particles are the stars of the show, while fields quietly provide the essential backdrop for everything that happens. Understanding their relationship helps us see why fields also deserve a round of applause.

Let's break it down. When we talk about particles, we usually think of the tiny building blocks of matter—like electrons, protons, neutrons, and their quirky cousins.

These are the characters that jump out at us, like rock stars delivering their biggest hits. But the real magic occurs with the fields that fill the universe, creating a stage for these particles to perform their dance. Think of fields as the backstage crew, making sure every particle has the perfect setting to shine.

Picture this: every time you pop open a can of soda, you're greeted by a fizzy explosion of bubbles. Those bubbles are like particles, bursting forth to grab your attention and tickle your taste buds. But what's really keeping those bubbles together? The soda itself, acting as a liquid field that allows the bubbles to exist. Without the soda, the bubbles would be nothing but a fleeting thought, floating aimlessly in the air. This leads us to our first funny analogy: particles are like bubbles in a can of soda, dependent on their surrounding fields to take shape and thrive.

Now, think about your favorite cooking show. What's the first thing the host usually does? They gather a mix of ingredients, each with its own unique flavor, and then create something special. The final dishes that come out are like particles—visually stunning and often the highlight of the episode. But the true artistry lies in how those ingredients work together, just like fields that combine to create an amazing outcome. In the kitchen, just as in the universe, every ingredient plays a vital role in the end result. Whether it's the garlic, the herbs, or the salt, they all need to come together harmoniously, just like fields must interact for particles to emerge.

To really understand how particles and fields interact, let's dive a bit deeper. In the vastness of space, fields stretch across every inch of the universe like an unseen quilt, with each fold representing a different type of field. For instance, the electromagnetic field governs how charged particles interact, while the gravitational field determines how objects with mass attract each other. Without these vital fields, particles would have nowhere to play; they'd be like performers lost in a crowd, unable to find their way to the stage.

Now, let's sprinkle in some humor, shall we? Imagine a packed coffee shop, where everyone is busy sipping lattes and tapping away on their laptops. Among the hustle and bustle, there's a barista skillfully navigating through the crowd. In this scenario, the barista is like the quantum field, managing the flow of interactions while the coffee drinkers are the particles, popping up and engaging with one another, creating a vibrant atmosphere. The coffee beans, the milk, the sugar—they all play a crucial role in crafting the perfect brew, just like fields give life to particles.

But the connection between particles and fields goes beyond simple interactions. Things get really interesting when we think about the phenomena that come from these fields. Imagine a well-timed joke at a party that has everyone in stitches. Just like laughter can ripple through a crowd, particles can appear and disappear as fluctuations in the fields happen. This playful unpredictability is a hallmark of quantum mechanics, where the usual rules seem to twist and turn in surprising ways, much like a prepared speech veering into a spontaneous improv comedy routine.

So, how can we capture this dynamic between particles and fields in a way that's both fun and enlightening? Let's visualize it this way: think of each field as an artist's canvas, and the particles as the vibrant brushstrokes that bring a painting to life. You might notice a stunning sunset, but without the canvas beneath it, those colors would have nowhere to flourish. The celestial dance of particles fully relies on the fields that support them, creating a breathtaking masterpiece of existence.

As we explore this quantum performance further, let's not forget that fields aren't just passive backgrounds for particles. They actively shape and influence how particles behave, sometimes in subtle, yet powerful ways. Imagine a crowded dance floor where someone accidentally steps on your toes while showing off their moves. The immediate pain you feel isn't just from the foot (the particle) but also from the energy of the dance floor (the field). In the same way, fields guide the actions and movements of particles, creating the rich landscape of the universe.

Take a moment to think about what this relationship means. When we view fields as active participants in the cosmic performance, we gain a deeper appreciation for their role in our reality. Suddenly, particles aren't just isolated entities; they're part of a grander scheme, an extensive network of connections where every action counts. It's as if we've been given exclusive backstage access to a magnificent show, gaining insights into the symphony of existence that unfolds every second, influencing everything from the tiniest electron to the largest galaxies.

In addition to these captivating comparisons, it's important to highlight how this interplay reveals the fundamental forces that shape our universe. Gravity can be thought of like a magnetic force pulling everything closer, while the electromagnetic field plays a game of attraction and repulsion, much like friends trying to navigate a tight circle on the dance floor. This complex choreography of interactions results in the universe we know, where energy flows like an unstoppable river, continually shaping the fabric of reality.

Understanding the relationship between particles and fields invites us to rethink our place within this cosmic performance. Just like each dancer contributes to the overall vibe of the party, every particle plays an important role in the grand choreography of existence. The relentless energy of the quantum field pulses through everything, reminding us that we're not just spectators; we're vital participants in this dance.

So, the next time you gaze up at the stars or ponder the mysteries of the universe, remember that we are all dancers on this grand cosmic stage, grooving to the rhythm of life's unpredictable yet beautiful tune. Embracing this idea lets us appreciate the deep complexities of quantum mechanics and encourages us to navigate life's twists and turns with laughter, curiosity, and a sense of connection to the world around us.

As we continue this journey into the quantum realm, let's keep in mind the vibrant relationship between particles and fields. The universe isn't just a collection of isolated bits; it's a complex web of energy vibrations, each contributing to the dance of existence. The quantum field isn't just a distant concept from textbooks; it's a lively and essential part of our reality, waiting for us to step onto its stage.

So let's celebrate this playful rivalry as we recognize the dynamic connection between particles and fields. Together, they create a dance of existence that is as enchanting as it is intricate. With humor and curiosity as our guiding lights, we can embrace the mysteries of the quantum world and open ourselves up to the delightful surprises that lie ahead. After all, life is too short to watch from the sidelines when the cosmic dance floor is beckoning us to join in.

Everything is Interconnected

Imagine a lively city square on a sunny Saturday, filled with laughter and chatter. Each person brings their own unique stories and experiences, mingling with those around them.

Picture someone dropping a coin; it rolls across the cobblestones and captures the attention of a nearby child, who eagerly bends down to pick it up. This tiny, seemingly unimportant act sets off a chain reaction: the child lets out a joyful squeal, which catches the ear of a musician nearby, prompting them to start playing a cheerful tune. In just a few moments, the square transforms from a collection of strangers into a vibrant community, where every interaction creates a beautiful web of connection.

Now, let's take a quick trip into the world of quantum physics—yes, the same realm where tiny particles dance and invisible fields ripple all around us. Just like our bustling city square, the universe operates on a principle of interconnectedness. It's a network where nothing stands alone. Just as one person's actions can spread joy to others, every particle is influenced by the surrounding fields around it. This creates a lively interplay that shapes everything we know in our universe.

To really understand this connection, let's look at social media as an example. Think about how a single tweet can reach people all over the world, sparking trends, memes, and discussions that spread like waves across the digital space. One person's casual comment can snowball into a global sensation, just like a shift in a quantum field can impact countless particles and lead to surprising outcomes.

Let's break this down a bit more. Imagine scrolling through your feed and coming across a meme that perfectly captures your current mood. You chuckle and hit the share button. Suddenly, your friend sees it, laughs, and shares it with their own network. Before you know it, that meme has crossed borders, evolving along the way—some might add a witty caption, while others might remix it with new images or references. The original joke expands and takes on new layers of meaning as it travels.

In the same way, particles exist within fields that are always buzzing with activity. When something changes—like a shift in temperature or a magnetic pull—these fluctuations ripple through the field. Particles respond, appearing or disappearing in a way that mimics how online trends evolve. A small change can lead to big effects, shaping interactions and outcomes that may seem totally unpredictable.

Now, let's take a light-hearted detour. Think of a hilarious viral video of a cat playing the piano. It all starts with a curious cat tapping at the keys, and before long, everyone, including your grandma, is sharing it online. What began as a simple display of feline curiosity becomes a cultural moment, inspiring remixes, parodies, and endless memes. This is the magic of our interconnected online world, where one adorable cat can lead to an entire universe of content.

Now, let's connect this to the concept of quantum entanglement. In this intriguing phenomenon, particles become linked in such a way that the state of one instantly influences the state of another, no matter how far apart they are. Think of two friends on opposite sides of the globe sharing a special bond. You know that feeling when your phone buzzes and you reach for it just as they send you a message? That's entanglement—it's that instant connection that defies distance.

To illustrate this even further, let's go back to our social media example. Picture two users, one in Tokyo and the other in New York. They've never met, but they both love the same obscure band. One day, the New Yorker posts an old concert clip that floods them with nostalgia, and, unbeknownst to them, the Tokyoite is watching it at the exact same moment. They both feel a spark of joy from that shared memory, despite being thousands of miles apart. This instant connection mirrors how entangled particles interact in the quantum world, where one action can influence another in real time, transcending space and time.

To make things even more fun, let's sprinkle in some humor. Imagine a scenario where every time you share a post raving about your love for tacos, that craving echoes through the universe. Your friends, feeling the delicious pull of your taco enthusiasm, suddenly find themselves at the nearest taco truck, devouring al pastor like there's no tomorrow. This is a light-hearted take on interconnectedness, illustrating how our thoughts and actions can create ripples in ways we might never expect.

Yet, amidst all the laughter, there's something beautifully profound about the interconnectedness of the universe. Realizing that we are all pieces of a grand puzzle—a cosmic jigsaw—can spark a sense of wonder and humility. Just like every tweet, meme, or shared taco craving intertwines with someone's life, every particle in the universe plays a role in the larger story of existence.

Think about it this way: if you've ever been at a concert and felt a wave of energy flow through the crowd, you know the beauty of interconnectedness. One person starts clapping, and soon, the entire audience is caught up in a rhythmic celebration. This is like how energy flows through quantum fields—each particle reacting to its neighbors, creating an electric atmosphere that everyone can feel.

In our daily lives, it's easy to overlook these connections. Social media, with all its quirks, reminds us of our shared experiences. Whether it's finding comfort in a viral dance challenge or bonding over mutual interests, these connections create a sense of belonging. In the quantum world, particles are not lonely entities drifting through space. Instead, they are engaged in a cosmic dance, constantly interacting with each other and their fields, shaping the universe in ways that often leave us in awe.

But let's not forget that life can sometimes feel like a game of telephone. One person shares a message, and by the time it reaches the last person in the line, it has changed completely. The same can happen in the quantum world, where interactions can lead to unexpected outcomes. A tiny shift in a field can produce a particle that behaves in surprising ways.

Remember that one friend who decided to change the lyrics to a popular song during karaoke? What started as a simple rendition turned into a hilarious medley that had everyone laughing. The quantum world is full of such playful surprises, where particles can act in bewildering ways, making us giggle and scratch our heads in equal measure.

When we reflect on the beauty of interconnectedness, let's embrace the delightful chaos. Just as every interaction on social media adds to the colorful mosaic of our online lives, every event in the quantum realm contributes to the vibrant story of existence. Each particle, like a unique social media post, holds its own importance, and together, they create a universe filled with diversity and spontaneity.

In a world that can sometimes feel divided, recognizing that we are all part of this interconnected web can fill us with hope. Every action we take sends ripples through the cosmic fabric, reminding us that we are not alone. Just as a tweet can inspire a movement, our actions can create change in ways we might not expect, showcasing the beauty of unity and teamwork.

So, as we keep exploring this fascinating idea of interconnectedness, let's embrace the shared chaos of our lives. Whether it's the laughter of friends, the joy of discovering a new meme, or the subtle shifts of quantum particles, these moments remind us that we are all part of something bigger. This web of life encourages us to appreciate the connections we make and the impact we have on each other.

Next time you scroll through your social media feed or find yourself lost in thought, pause for a moment to consider the invisible threads that link us all. Just as particles can spark reactions and create ripples in the quantum realm, our everyday interactions shape the world around us. Life is a wonderfully chaotic dance, and we are all participants, connected in this extraordinary experience.

By understanding our interconnectedness, we can develop a deeper appreciation for the complexity of life. It's a reminder that every small action, every shared laugh, and every taco craving indulged enriches the larger narrative of existence. So let's move forward with joy, curiosity, and open hearts, ready to embrace the delightful unpredictability of the world around us. After all, in this vast universe, we are all dancers in the grand cosmic performance, tied together by the threads of laughter, love, and shared experiences.

Chapter 10: Quantum Weirdness: Embracing the Chaos

Imagine stepping into a lively room full of people laughing and chatting away, only to realize you're the only one who can't quite grasp what's going on. You drift around, trying to catch bits of conversation, but every time you focus on one group, the others fade into the background. Welcome to the curious party that is quantum physics! In this wild world, the rules are far from clear-cut.

Quantum mechanics is like that playful friend who enjoys pulling pranks. Just when you think you've got it figured out—BAM!—it surprises you. One moment, you think you understand how particles work, and then you learn they can act like waves. Just when you think you've grasped that wave-particle duality, you stumble upon the observer effect, which tells us that simply observing something can actually influence its behavior. It's as if the universe is cheekily saying, "Gotcha!"

At the core of quantum mechanics is the idea of wave-particle duality. Light, which we usually think of as tiny particles called photons, also behaves like a wave. Think of it like a quirky film festival: one minute, you're watching a heartwarming rom-com, and the next you're plunged into an abstract art piece that leaves you puzzled. This wave-particle puzzle is similar to trying to decide if your favorite meme features a sad dog or a confused cat; it all depends on how you look at it in that moment.

Next up is the well-known observer effect. Let's break this down: imagine it like a reality TV show. Whenever you tune in, the contestants start acting differently. Close your eyes, and they might just go back to their true, chaotic selves! In quantum physics, it's not just about looking at particles; the very act of measuring them can change their state. So, the next time you find yourself in a tricky situation, consider standing back and letting things unfold without your watchful gaze.

Now, how do we make sense of these playful ideas? One way is through the fun world of memes and analogies. For example, think about Schrödinger's cat, a thought experiment that captures the heart of quantum superposition. Here, a cat is both dead and alive until someone takes a peek inside the box. It's like living in a constant state of "Will they? Won't they?" that keeps you guessing. The duality of the cat's fate offers a fascinating way to understand how different realities can exist together until we make a decision—or in this case, lift the lid.

Humor gives us a special way to connect with these seemingly odd concepts. It's easy to feel overwhelmed by the tricky nature of quantum mechanics, but when we sprinkle in some lightheartedness, those daunting ideas become a lot easier to digest. Take the Heisenberg Uncertainty Principle, for instance. It tells us that you can't know both the exact position and momentum of a particle at the same time. Imagine your life as a juggling act: you can either focus on the ball (position) or on how fast it's moving (momentum), but trying to do both is nearly impossible. This playful image helps clarify the idea of uncertainty in quantum physics.

Quantum physics is packed with paradoxes that can tickle your brain in the most delightful ways. Take the double-slit experiment, for example. When particles are shot at a barrier with two slits, they create an interference pattern that suggests they're acting like waves. But when you observe them, the particles choose a slit, behaving like particles once again. It's the ultimate game of peekaboo; the moment you look, they change how they perform. It's as if the universe is winking at us, saying, "I'm here, but only if you're not watching!"

As we dive deeper into the antics of quantum particles, we start to see that accepting uncertainty can uncover unexpected discoveries in our lives. Just like in quantum mechanics, sometimes our best moments happen when we least expect them. The unpredictability of life is much like the randomness of particles; it's less about controlling every outcome and more about enjoying the journey. Picture yourself on a rollercoaster, hands in the air, embracing every twist and turn. The excitement comes not from knowing what's next, but from relishing the thrilling surprises along the way.

And let's not forget about entanglement, which is perhaps the most mind-blowing part of quantum mechanics. Imagine two particles that become connected in such a way that the state of one instantly affects the other, no matter how far apart they are. This phenomenon reflects the saying, "Out of sight, but not out of mind." It's like having a cosmic best friend who knows when you're in trouble, even if they're light-years away.

When we welcome the weirdness of quantum physics, we start to see the beauty in chaos. Just as quantum mechanics challenges our traditional ideas of reality, our own lives are filled with surprises and unexpected paths. Learning to laugh at the absurdity of it all can help us navigate the uncertainties we face.

In summary, the world of quantum mechanics serves as a playful reminder of the unpredictable nature of existence. It encourages us to keep our minds open, our hearts light, and to recognize that sometimes the best way to tackle the unknown is with a good laugh and a willingness to embrace the chaos. So, as we wander through the maze of quantum oddities, let's hold onto the cosmic joke and remember that life, like the universe, is a grand adventure packed with surprises just waiting to be found.

Trolled by the Universe

Welcome to the vibrant world of quantum physics, where particles seem to dance to a rhythm known only to them, and the normal rules of reality take a break. If you've ever felt like the universe was having a laugh at your expense, you're definitely not alone. Quantum mechanics is like the universe's playful trickster, tossing around strange puzzles that leave even the brightest minds scratching their heads. So, grab some snacks and get comfy, because we're about to dive into a fun exploration of some of the most famous thought experiments in quantum physics. Get ready for a journey where cats can be both alive and dead, and particles appear to chat with each other across huge distances!

Let's kick things off with the famous Schrödinger's cat. Picture this: a cat cozying up inside a box, completely unaware of its fate. Next to it is a vial of poison, which is triggered by a quantum event involving a radioactive atom. If the atom decays, the cat meets a sad end; if it doesn't, our furry friend keeps snoozing happily. Here's the unusual twist: until someone opens the box to take a peek, the cat is both alive and dead at the same time. This strange scenario captures the essence of quantum uncertainty perfectly.

Now, let's put on our creative thinking caps and imagine that this cat is actually a party planner. Yes, you heard me right! While the poor kitty is stuck in a state of suspense, it's also busy dreaming up the most amazing party of the year. Friends from both the living and the dead are on the guest list, and the invitations have already been sent. The cat is blissfully unaware of the stakes at hand; it's caught up in themes, colors, and cake flavors. Should it choose tuna-flavored cupcakes or chicken pâté cookies? Now that's a tough call, and it makes for a delightful mess.

The moment you lift the lid, everything changes. The cat's fate is now sealed, and it can no longer plan its big bash. This thought experiment, while deeply philosophical, shines a light on the silliness of trying to understand a universe that seems to chuckle at our attempts to make sense of it. In many ways, we're all like Schrödinger's cat, juggling different possibilities in our lives while trying to keep afloat in a sea of chaos. So whether you're planning a surprise party or just figuring out what to wear tomorrow, remember that uncertainty is something we all share; it's always lurking around, ready to throw a surprise your way.

Next up is the legendary double-slit experiment, a classic that highlights the quirky behavior of particles. Imagine this: scientists shine a beam of particles at a screen with two slits. When no one is watching, the particles create a beautiful interference pattern, acting like waves and leaving peaks and troughs on the screen behind. It's like watching a stunning dance performance where the dancers move in perfect harmony, blending into one another. The performance is awe-inspiring, and you can't help but feel captivated by its beauty.

But as soon as someone decides to take a peek—yes, just the act of observing—the game changes completely. The particles suddenly behave like separate little beings, choosing one slit or the other, and that lovely interference pattern vanishes. It's almost as if the particles are saying, "Oh, you're watching? Well, we'll behave ourselves now." Imagine the universe pulling a clever trick on us, like a playful puppeteer, reminding us that sometimes, not knowing can feel like a blessing.

The double-slit experiment offers a humorous glimpse into the nature of reality itself. It raises questions about the role of the observer—do we really have the power to shape what we see? It's a bit like catching your friend doing something silly; the moment they realize they're being watched, their charm just evaporates. When you notice, the spontaneous fun disappears, and they become their usual, self-aware selves again. The universe, it seems, loves a good show.

Now, let's chat about quantum entanglement, perhaps one of the most mind-blowing concepts in quantum physics. Imagine two particles that become so closely linked that whatever happens to one instantly impacts the other, no matter the distance. It's as if these particles share a cosmic connection, a bond that goes beyond space and time. Picture them as two best friends living on opposite sides of the world, finishing each other's sentences. One sends a message, and the other instantly knows how to respond, as if connected by an invisible line of communication.

This phenomenon is so strange that Einstein called it "spooky action at a distance." Yet, it beautifully reminds us of how interconnected we all are, even when we don't notice it. Think about your own friendships. Have you ever felt that something was up with a friend, even when they were far away? Or maybe you and your best friend sent each other the same meme at the same time? That's what friendship-level entanglement feels like—a joyful connection that can seem to defy the laws of physics.

While quantum mechanics might seem like a cosmic trickster, it reveals a much deeper truth about our existence. Life is full of contradictions and surprises, and it often throws us curveballs just when we think we have it all figured out. Embracing the quirks of quantum physics encourages us to accept the oddities in our own lives. In a world that often feels divided, recognizing our interconnectedness can be a truly uplifting realization.

As we navigate through the puzzling realms of quantum mechanics, we find that humor can light our way. The absurdity of Schrödinger's cat, the playful nature of the double-slit experiment, and the magical bond of entangled particles all showcase the whimsical side of reality. It's perfectly okay to feel a bit overwhelmed, to have a good laugh, and to marvel at the mysteries just beyond our reach. Just like the universe, our lives are full of unexpected events, odd turns, and delightful surprises.

So let's embrace the chaos together! Life, much like quantum physics, is an exciting adventure filled with unanticipated moments. Whether it's a cat waiting in a box, particles playing peekaboo, or friends who inexplicably know each other's thoughts, there's beauty in all this unpredictability. The next time you're grappling with uncertainty, remember that the universe is probably chuckling along with you, reminding you that it's all part of the cosmic joke. And who knows? Maybe getting a grasp on the quirks of quantum physics will help you navigate your own life's puzzles with a bit more ease and humor. So go ahead, lift that box, and welcome the universe's playful spirit into your life!

Quantum Physics as Life's Meme

Imagine standing at a crossroads, your heart racing and your mind buzzing with possibilities. It feels like you're peering into a wild universe, much like quantum physics itself. The uncertainty principle, a key idea in quantum mechanics introduced by Werner Heisenberg, resonates in our daily lives: "The more precisely the position is determined, the less precisely the momentum is known, and vice versa." This means the harder we try to control our lives, the more we wrestle with uncertainty, often leading us to laugh at the absurdity of it all. It's like the universe has a sense of humor, and it's perfectly okay to enjoy the ride.

As we move through the unpredictable landscape of everyday life, it's hard not to see parallels with the quirky rules of quantum physics. Just like particles that refuse to be pinned down to one state, our lives often seem to exist in a state of possibility, bursting with different potential outcomes. Picture this:

when you walk into a coffee shop, you weigh your options—should you go for a caffeine kick or stick with herbal tea? Scone or muffin? Each choice represents a different reality, and until you make that decision, they all coexist in your mind. Isn't that a fun way to look at the chaos of daily decision-making?

Let's take a moment to share a memory of a cooking mishap that transformed into a delightful success. I remember one time when I attempted to bake a simple vanilla cake. The plan seemed clear-cut, but somehow, between measuring the flour and whisking the eggs, I got a bit lost. Instead of adding one cup of sugar, I accidentally dumped in an entire bag! I thought there was no way to save it, so I poured the batter into a pan and slid it into the oven, half-expecting a complete flop.

But when the timer went off and I opened the door, the scent that filled the air was incredible. What came out wasn't a disaster but a dreamy creation—sweet, moist, and absolutely delightful. Friends who tasted it raved about my "signature dish," and I couldn't help but chuckle at the irony: sometimes, things can turn out wonderfully, even when we try so hard to control them. Just like particles in quantum mechanics that surprise us, life often brings unexpected joys.

To embrace the unpredictable, let's explore a few "Quantum Life Lessons," each paired with a playful meme that captures the silliness of our existence.

1. **Embrace Uncertainty**: Life is like a buffet of options, and you often won't know what you'll get until you dig in. Sometimes, the best flavors come from surprising combinations. [*Picture of a confused cat staring at an open fridge, pondering life's choices*]
2. **Superposition is Your Friend**: Just like Schrödinger's cat, you can exist in more than one state at once. You can be "focused on work" while also "daydreaming about pizza." [*Image of a cat in a box, half studying, half dreaming of pizza*]
3. **Control is an Illusion**: We can plan all we want, but the universe loves to throw curveballs. Acknowledge the chaos and just roll with it. [*Meme of a cat wearing a helmet on a rollercoaster, looking thrilled*]
4. **Quantum Leaps are Just That**: Life is full of surprises. Take that leap of faith; you might just land on the moon—or at

least on the couch with a bag of chips. [*Image of an excited cat leaping toward a couch*]

5. **Laughter is Universal**: Much like quantum entanglement, laughter connects us all. Share a joke and watch the distance between you and others shrink. [*Meme of two cats sharing a joke, laughing together*]

These quirky lessons encourage us to approach life with a sense of humor. By infusing humor into our daily experiences, we create a bridge between the puzzling world of quantum physics and our everyday challenges. It teaches us that the unknown isn't something to fear; rather, it's an opportunity for growth, laughter, and connection.

The beauty of quantum physics and its inherent chaos encourages us to loosen our grip on the need for absolute certainty. When you think about it, our lives are filled with experiments—some succeed, others flop, and many fall somewhere in between. Just like particles that remain uncertain until they're observed, we often discover that our paths become clearer when we embrace the unknown. Each unplanned moment can lead to joy, excitement, and laughter.

Think of a family gathering where someone is supposed to bring a dish. Rather than sticking to a tried-and-true recipe, they decide to experiment with something completely new. The outcome? A culinary mishap that turns into the highlight of the evening, sparking laughter and stories. Everyone bonds over the shared silliness of it all, and what could have been embarrassing transforms into a beloved memory. In life, just like in quantum physics, the unexpected can lead to the most rewarding outcomes.

In this playful quantum world, there's a vital lesson in being adaptable. When we accept chaos and acknowledge that things might not go as planned, we become more open and resilient. It's a little like how quantum particles change their behavior when observed. Our ability to pivot allows us to find joy in surprise and discover deeper meaning in life's chaotic moments.

Sometimes, it helps to visualize these ideas through humor and relatable stories. Imagine a day when everything seems to go wrong. You spill coffee on your shirt, miss the bus, and get caught in the rain without an umbrella. By the end of the day, you're soaked and out of sorts, but then you stumble upon a street performer strumming a ukulele. You pause, listen, and suddenly find yourself smiling despite the day's mishaps. In that moment, the laughter and music remind you that even in chaos, there's beauty to be appreciated. It's a spontaneous connection, much like quantum entanglement, where joy bridges gaps between us.

  As we journey through life, the key is to stay curious. Instead of viewing uncertainty as a weight, let's approach it with the mindset of a scientist, eager to learn and explore. The next time you face an unexpected twist, ask yourself: What can I learn from this? How can I find joy in the absurd? Embracing each moment with curiosity transforms our experiences from mere events into memorable tales.

  Imagine waking up one morning with everything planned out perfectly. You have a to-do list, meetings lined up, and a well-organized schedule. But as the day unfolds, one hiccup after another throws your plans off course. Instead of getting frustrated, find humor in the situation. Maybe you miss an important meeting but end up at an impromptu yoga class where you discover a hidden love for downward dog. Life has a knack for redirecting us, and when we allow ourselves to be adaptable, we can uncover delightful surprises tucked within the chaos.

In the grand scheme of things, understanding quantum physics can inspire us to rethink how we relate to uncertainty. By lifting the lid off our metaphorical boxes, we make room for adventure, spontaneity, and a dash of humor in our lives. Embracing the quirks of existence—both in quantum mechanics and our daily choices—allows us to cultivate a mindset that welcomes the unexpected.

Ultimately, quantum physics reminds us that our lives aren't meant to follow a strict script. Just like particles that dance through the universe without a care, we too can find joy in life's unpredictable twists and turns. By opening ourselves up to the surprises that come our way, we cultivate a sense of wonder that enriches our experiences and helps us navigate the delightful chaos of the universe.

As we wrap up our exploration of the intriguing world of quantum physics, let's carry these insights forward. Let's recognize the humor in life's unpredictability and celebrate those absurd moments that remind us we're all part of a larger cosmic joke. By embracing uncertainty, we build resilience, laughter, and a sense of community—reminders that we're all connected, even when we feel adrift in a sea of possibilities.

So, the next time you find yourself facing an unexpected challenge, take a deep breath, laugh at the irony, and dive into whatever absurdity lies ahead. Just like the particles in a quantum experiment, you might find that the unknown leads to the most thrilling adventures, surprising connections, and unforgettable moments. Embrace the chaos, because it's in this delightful uncertainty that life truly unfolds.

Conclusion

As we wrap up our quantum comedy tour, remember: the universe is weird, wonderful, and full of surprises. We've laughed our way through entanglement, superposition, and even gave Schrödinger's cat a break (it's probably grateful).

You've now got the tools to see the world through quantum-tinted glasses. So go forth and spread the joy of quantum physics! Share a meme about wave functions, crack a joke about quantum tunneling, or simply ponder the possibility that you're simultaneously reading this conclusion and not reading it in another universe.

Keep exploring, keep questioning, and most importantly, keep laughing. After all, in the grand quantum comedy club of the universe, we're all just particles trying to make sense of the cosmic punchline.

Theodore Trudeau

Printed in Dunstable, United Kingdom